The Impossible Life

The Impossible Life

by Jesse Enns

The Impossible Life $12.95

Copyright ©2022 by Jesse Enns

To contact the author, please write to the below postal or email address:

Christians for Messiah Ministries

PO Box 36324

Rock Hill, SC 29732

Email: jesse@aicchurch.com

All scriptures taken from the New International Version unless otherwise noted.
Scriptures taken from the Holy Bible, New International Version ©

All rights reserved. No part of this publication may be reproduced without prior permission of Christians for Messiah Publishing or Jesse Enns

First Christians for Messiah Ministries edition published 2022

Cover Design by: Rebecca Barrett

Editing by: Peter Wyns, Bethany Ritter, Lisa Antonson

Manufactured in the United States of America by Ingram Spark

ISBN: 978-1-7355929-4-7

Dedication

I dedicate this book to the love of my life, Elizabeth. Your relentless pursuit of God has been my inspiration. I love living life with you - and I really like you.

Table of Contents

Introduction	ix
Chapter 1: All In	1
Chapter 2: Abandonment	9
Chapter 3: Expensive Love	19
Chapter 4: Beyond Belief	27
Chapter 5: Overcoming Faith	37
Chapter 6: Death of a Seed	47
Chapter 7: It's About Time	57
Chapter 8: The Heart of the Matter	67
Chapter 9: Fruitfulness	75
Chapter 10: Humility and Success	85
Chapter 11: You Can't Go It Alone	93
Chapter 12: Life in the Spirit	101

Introduction

In the fall of 2021, God began to speak to us about Elizabeth, my wife, running for political office. Like most things God calls us to do, the math didn't seem to add up. We lacked the time, the finances, the name recognition, and the experience. Not only that, but we weren't even interested in that depth of involvement. We were already very busy, pastoring a growing church, raising our three boys, and were heavily involved with a handful of other regional and national endeavors. Surely there was someone else qualified who could run for political office. But my wife had prayed a dangerous prayer about a year before that. She said, "Lord, whatever doors you open, I will walk through." That began a very unexpected season of initiatives that propelled us into realms and places that we never thought we would be in.

By the spring of 2022, we were in full swing in a competitive political campaign (for the South Carolina state house) when God spoke to me and told me that it was time to write this book. "Wait, now??? I don't have time for that!" was my reply. I was already running a million miles an hour trying to hold everything together between pastoring the church and being Elizabeth's political campaign manager. We had a limited amount of time to knock on 3,000 doors, make 5,000 phone calls, manage several mail pieces, social media posts, and raise an enormous amount of funds. I couldn't afford to take a few hours off, let alone a few days, to begin writing a book on the impossible life. Then God reminded me of the title of the book and the theme that He had given me to write about. He said, "If you can't do the impossible, how are you going to write about the impossible?" Sufficiently corrected, I accepted the challenge and began unpacking what God had given me. I trusted the God of all power to strengthen me in my lack. I gave Him my 'Yes,' just like my wife had, and trusted that even if I couldn't hold it all together, He could – and would.

The themes I share in this book are very much grounded in real-life experiences. God has shown Himself faithful and true in every season of my life. My desire for this book is that it propels you forward to see what a life yielded to Jesus Christ can look like. Each one of us is on a different journey, and the fruit in our lives will be unique to the seasons we are in and the calling He has given. However, we all serve the same God who does

Introduction

the impossible, and His plans include more than just improving our lives. He wants to completely rearrange our lives so that we experience the true life that only He can give. It's all part of His eternal plan. The sooner we get on board with His plans, the sooner we find ourselves engulfed in Heaven's supernatural power and purpose. Once you taste this kind of life, this kind of adventure, nothing else will satisfy your soul. So, I invite you to join me on a journey unlike any other; God is calling you into the realm of radical trust and living for Him. Take off your seatbelt and prepare to experience a world without physical restraints. I welcome you to the supernatural. I welcome you to the Impossible Life.

CHAPTER 1

All In

Every year, the hill behind our elementary school would be covered in snow. Much bigger than the little slope that you are likely picturing in your mind, this was a small mountain. At every lunch and recess, we would head to the top of the hill with our sleds. My favorite vehicle of choice was a GT Snowracer. It had two skis underneath a long seat and a single ski in front, controlled by a steering wheel. There were brakes in the form of notched metal plates that you press to slow yourself down, but, being a 12-year-old boy, I had removed those off my sled, as most of my friends had done to theirs. We didn't need brakes – we wanted speed! We had such a blast making jumps at the bottom of the hill and seeing how much air we could get.

One year, a massive pile of dirt was brought in for landscaping, and then it snowed. The huge dirt pile was perfectly placed at the bottom of the hill and created the most incredible jump we had ever seen. It was over 10 feet high and looked like a snowy volcano. My friend and I decided to be the first to fly off Mount Snowvius! We climbed the big hill, GT Snowracer in tow. This sled could fit two on it, and I was the passenger this time. About 200 feet of steep descent, followed by a 10-foot vertical jump, was what awaited us. We took our positions; I wrapped my arms around his waist, took a deep breath, and pushed off; there was no stopping us. We hurtled down the hill at what seemed like breakneck speed. All the kids were cheering and hollering as we sped down the big hill until we reached the snow-covered dirt pile. We ascended its snowy banks at full speed and hit the top. And then ... silence.

We went soaring through the air at an incredible height. Suddenly, all the hustle and bustle of the kids stopped as every eye was fixed on our flying sled. As we flew through the air, the only sound I could hear was the wind whistling by my ears. We finally hit the ground and totally bailed. The sled landed slightly sideways, and we tipped over. We lay on the ground as all the kids around us yelled out in exuberant amazement about the distance we had just flown. My friend and I remained motionless in the snow, not saying a word. As kids came rushing towards us to congratulate us, we realized the impact of our landing had knocked the wind out of us, so we couldn't speak. We just smiled at one another as the crowd of kids surrounded us. Finally, our strength and breath returned, and we stood up and celebrated as victorious overcomers. We measured the distance of our jump at more than 20 feet. It was a new personal best and a new world record – at least as far as we were concerned.

There comes a point in any adventure when you have to commit. Some call it the point of no return. For us, in this particular instance, that moment was at the very start of our journey - because we had ripped the brakes off our sled. Whatever adventure you are destined for, there comes that deep breath before the plunge, where you have to commit; you have to go all in. This is what the Christian journey is meant to look like – we are to fly in the purposes of God – but it doesn't just happen. It requires an ongoing commitment to live beyond the borders of our will, minds, and comfort zones.

The Christian walk is an all-in endeavor. Like a good marriage, it will cost you your life. Of course, those with experience can testify that this is not a one-and-done process either. Paul said, "I die daily." 1 Cor. 15:31

Even Jesus said that disciples are required to take up their cross daily and follow Him. However, there's a big difference between all dead and mostly dead (as any fan of the Princess Bride movie will know). Mostly dead is still slightly alive.

But life is life, and death is death – both are absolute terms; the contrast is stark! We are meant to live all in! Jesus didn't come so that you might have a little bit of life, a little infusion for an acceptable existence. No, He said He came to give us abundant, overflowing life (see John 10:10). If that's why Jesus came, the question remains, are we living this abundant life? Or are we shortchanging the experience of God in our lives? Every believer is invited to go on this adventure, but it requires that we are all in.

If we want to enter into this abundant life, it stands to reason that we must live according to the design of the One who created it for us. If we fail to understand the rules, we won't be able to win the prize. Scripture says, "No one serving as a soldier gets entangled in civilian affairs, but rather tries to please his commanding officer. Similarly, anyone who competes as an athlete does not receive the victor's crown except by competing according to the rules." 2 Tim. 2:3-5

Too many of us run aimlessly or without the proper understanding or motivation to run and win the prize. Because of our temporal worldview, when we don't see an attainable prize, we lose the motivation to run. I remember being told that I had to run in a 400m race for my school. The problem was I was a natural sprinter (100m and 200m). I had never run a 400m race.

Nevertheless, I found myself in the starting blocks. The gun sounded, and off I went. After I was about halfway through the race, several runners had already crossed the finish line – and the nearest person in front of me was almost 100 yards ahead. I kept running but started waving to the crowd, hoping to at least make people laugh with me instead of just at me. I finished last and was promptly reprimanded by my coach for making a mockery of the race. I had lost the motivation to try my best and give it my all because the prize was not attainable.

This seems like the condition of the Church today. So many believers are running the race but are either ill-equipped or untrained and therefore the prize (at least in this life) seems unattainable. Of course, we believe in Heaven, and for that reason, most believers will continue to run, or at least walk, the race of faith, but not with all their hearts. There is, however, a reward available to us now. It's called the impossible life. The life that Christ offers does not just start when we go to heaven, but in order to walk in it and win the prize, we have to follow the rules. The rules tell us we must die to our fleshly desires and allow God to fill us with His life. If we don't like the rules and choose not to apply them, we lose the blessing. If we serve the God of the universe, who offers the impossible and supernatural life, then our lives should reflect it.

Life is seemingly unpredictable. The COVID-19 pandemic opened our eyes to see how temporary our daily lives and experiences are. As society seeks to pick up the pieces and move on from what seems like living in a bad movie, the people of God have an opportunity to kick into high gear and experience something new. What society has seen is not just a physical battle against a physical disease. It has come hand-in-hand with an emboldening of much darker spiritual forces, which are pulling down Biblical values in our culture. It's not enough to agree to disagree these days; instead, conformity is being demanded under threat of severe punishment, seeking to silence, shut down and even eliminate the Church, or anyone who speaks out against the progressive agenda that is sweeping the world. Now is not the time to dream about the good old days.

Christianity has always been destined for a collision course with the world. The kingdom of God is accelerating to ramming speed, as is the kingdom of darkness. It has always been that way. We just see it more clearly now, and we're past the point of no return. Believers who want to walk in step with God are being called out of their comfort zone as the darkness gets darker. I strongly suggest that now is a good time for Christians to take God at His word and go all in. God is looking for a people who will live the impossible life. He is looking for a people who are all in.

As we commit to this radical life, then God begins to work on our behalf. Scripture says, "For the eyes of the Lord range throughout the earth to strengthen those whose hearts are fully committed to him." 2 Chron. 16:19

God is actively seeking those who are willing to live this kind of life. There is a secret power that is released when you go all in, but you have to compete by the rules. You have to be on God's side. The Lord is with you when you are with Him.

The phrases "is with you" and "are with Him" are actually one word in Hebrew – the word *daresh*. It means to seek, enquire, or search. So, this verse could also be translated as: Seek God, and He will seek you. Enquire of God and He will enquire of you. Search for God and He will search for you. It's about a two-way covenant. It sums up what a covenant relationship with God looks like. The Lord is with you when you are with Him.

In other words, you can live your life in such a way that compels God to move on your behalf. Of course, we cannot manipulate or control God, but His promise to us says that if we live our lives totally for Him, then

He will give His life totally to us. The totality of the life that He offers can affect every area of our lives. It doesn't just mean going to church or reading our Bibles more. He wants all of it. For example, as a parent, it means you raise your kids in the fear of the Lord. In your relationships, it means you forgive, love, and learn to trust. In your faith walk, it means you go for God's best; you don't hold anything back. In your daily walk, it means trusting God for provision, wisdom, blessings, healing, supernatural power, and for the rewards that He promises to those who are all in. So, we begin this journey. It's not easy, but it is worth it.

It's time to leave the old, boring Christian walk behind. Forget normal life; Jesus didn't save you for a normal life. He died and lives forevermore to give you resurrection life, supernatural life, abundant life. It's available for you right now. All you have to do is go all in.

CHAPTER 2

Abandonment

One of the necessary ingredients to live the impossible life with God is the concept of abandonment. To accomplish something great often requires incredible focus, which means that other things, even good things, are pushed out of the way to make way for what is better. For example, a professional athlete must train in such a disciplined way. Their end goal determines how they live their lives. To succeed, they must commit to a lifestyle that restricts almost every detail of their lives – from diet and activities to their leisure time. To remain at the top of their game requires study, practice, discipline, hard work, and determination. Success is only possible through a high level of abandonment toward the goal they have set.

It's no different for those who want to live the impossible life. Many believers are content to live without the required sacrifices and settle for a seemingly basic Christian life. But as outlined in the previous chapter, the days are growing darker, and in time, the impossible nature of the Christian walk will become more and more appealing. Beyond that, it will become more and more necessary. We will need the power of the Gospel to affect and define every aspect of our lives when the collision of two spiritual kingdoms becomes unavoidable. Remember, God wants all of you so that He can give you all of Himself and you can experience the life He has for you. This level of abandonment to the things of the Lord is emphasized by Jesus when He says, "If anyone comes to me and does not hate father and mother, wife and children, brothers, and sisters—yes, even their own life—such a person cannot be my disciple." Luke 14:26

Jesus is not condoning hatred for the loved ones in our lives. That would be inconsistent with His other teachings. He is saying that if anything in our lives (including family) comes before Him, then we cannot properly receive the life He has for us. This all-encompassing life is only available to those who are dead to everything else. That's one of the reasons our salvation is called being 'born again.'

Abandonment means total trust or reckless indifference to the result. Thankfully, because we trust God (who leads us into all truth and who is the way, the truth, and the life), we are not reckless when we follow Him completely. After all, He is good and is more loving and caring for us and those in our lives than we are. So we have every reason to live with abandonment.

When I was a teenager growing up in the mountains of British Columbia, Canada, we would spend our summers at the lake. The dry, humid temperatures were perfectly complemented by the clean, cool lakes of the Okanagan Valley. As young people, one of our favorite spots was the cliffs. The landscape of the lakefront was filled with rock faces and deep water. There were three main cliffs. The beginner's cliff was about 23 feet high; the medium range was 40 feet high, and the highest cliff measured a whopping 100-foot drop. The most common spot, by far, was the beginner's cliff. There were a couple of protruding rocks below, but they only came out about 5 feet – which meant that with the slightest push-off, the jumper would safely land several feet past the rocks in the deep water below.

The thing about cliff jumping is that it requires a moment – a moment where sheer willpower and decisiveness transfer from your brain to the rest of your body. Some may argue that the brain is not involved in this process as much as it should be. Nevertheless, that moment of abandonment is required to instruct the body to leave the stability of the solid ground on which you stand and launch yourself into the unknown. After the first couple of times, the fear subsides, and sheer thrill and fun take over. I had a friend who would sit on the cliff's edge and just stare at the drop. For several minutes, he would try to conjure up the courage to make the leap. Getting up and breathing deeply, he would assume the jumping position, only to sit back down again and contemplate further. Meanwhile, the rest of us would be jumping off the cliff beside him, having a great time and telling him how fun it was. Half an hour would pass, and my friend would still be sitting there, thinking, gazing, wondering what it would be like.

After a long battle within him, he finally found the courage he needed. He stood up with conviction in his eyes, pushed back the argument in his head, and went through a couple of practice motions. His feet still did not want to move. They had grown somewhat accustomed to the security of the solid ground. But in one final moment of abandonment, he leaped off the cliff and plunged victoriously into the water below as the rest of us cheered and celebrated his act of bravery. He finally did it.

The thing about cliff jumping is that you can't keep one foot on the ground while the rest of you jumps. It requires total abandonment, a forsaking of other comforts or desires, to focus on what is needed to propel yourself forward.

In our walk with God, a similar process is required. We must choose to let go and let God. Letting go means not allowing the lawyer inside our head to argue us out of what we are about to do. You know the lawyer; it's that voice of rational thought which gives you every excuse why you shouldn't do it. That's the lawyer we must ignore when we take a leap of faith and obey the Lord. As we learn to trust God with our lives, it gets easier every time we jump.

Then, to our surprise, God calls us to jump off a higher cliff, and the lawyer comes roaring back. Theoretically, there's no difference between jumping 23 feet and 40 feet. The approach is the same; nothing has changed – except the height and our perspective. Forty feet looks *way* higher than twenty-three feet. So, we go through the process all over again. This happens each time God asks us to trust Him with another area of our lives. If we allow the Lord to teach us to live with abandonment, we learn to push through the trepidation and trust Him. I wonder if that's why scripture says to work out your salvation with fear and trembling (see Phil 2:12). God knows we are going to have to let go of our own desires and needs in order to fully trust Him with our future and our families, our career, calling, comfort, and even our lives.

About eight years ago, our church had outgrown our building. My wife and I were the associate pastors, along with her parents, who led as senior pastors. We had started the church together seven years prior, and it had grown to about 200 people, completely using up every chair in the room. We needed to find a new meeting place. After a couple of years of actively searching and trying various alternatives, nothing was forthcoming. God gave my father-in-law a dream about God expanding us as a church. He shared it with the church and told the congregation to pray. One month later, we were approached by the owner of a very large facility (the old PTL Barn and Studio in Fort Mill, SC – where Jim Bakker had his church and TV program in the 1980s). The facility was 2 acres under roof (over 100,000 square feet) and had 18 acres of land.

The owner offered to sell us the building for a discounted rate and hold the mortgage. This was a miracle, as no bank had been willing to work with us. We were considered a big risk to the banks. But God put it in the heart of this owner to offer the building to us. I was excited but acutely aware of how unrealistic this was for us. I was the church treasurer, the numbers guy, and I knew the numbers simply didn't add up. The new payment for the building and utilities was going to be *four* times what we brought in as income each month – not to mention the other ongoing expenses we had to factor in. God was asking us to take a leap.

I couldn't get my head around the numbers. The lawyer inside my head wouldn't stop presenting his case. But we knew God had spoken. He went on to confirm it with more dreams and words to various members of our congregation. But those members weren't in charge of the church's finances – I was. I felt responsible for ensuring we were not setting ourselves up to fail. My father-in-law sat down with me, and we talked about all the challenges and opportunities this would bring. He then said to me, "Jesse, I've never had a faith venture in God fail. But . . . if we do this, and it does fail, then you and I will just brush ourselves off, go out for dinner, and start again." His words seemed reckless. It's not that simple, is it? He knew that God had spoken, and His trust was in God, not in our bank account or financial history. It was enough to get me from sitting – to standing over the edge. I examined my heart and allowed faith to rise (not presumption – but faith that comes by hearing God's voice). With that, we took the leap.

We told our church congregation that it was a miracle the building came to us, and it would have to be a miracle every month to sustain us. It has now been over eight years into this miracle, and we haven't missed a beat. God has been faithful time after time. We had countless close calls and desperate moments where it seemed like it would all fall apart, but then God would provide in some unexpected way. There have been so many miracle moments, but God has been faithful to His word. It has become one of the most significant faith journeys of my life, and I wouldn't change it for the world.

But I would have missed it and all the blessings and growth opportunities that have come with it if I didn't allow the Lord to teach me how to pursue Him with this abandonment and trust Him with the results. Because if I want a life that experiences the supernatural power of God, then I will have to be in situations that are way beyond my ability to control or make happen. If it depends on me, then it's not good enough, not big enough, and will not ultimately satisfy the longings of my heart.

While in the dry and barren wilderness, King David put it this way: "You, God, are my God, earnestly I seek you; I thirst for you, my whole being longs for you, in a dry and parched land where there is no water." Psalm 63:1

David knew physical lack, but He knew that there was something better than physical refreshment – it was the life found in God Himself. In verse 3, he says "Because your love is better than life, my lips will glorify you."

That is the meaning of abandonment; understanding that the love of God, the nature of God, the care of God, the word of God, and the presence of God is better than life itself.

We must forsake the good to lay hold of what is better – and there's nothing better than Him. If we choose not to relinquish our claim to what is good in life, then we miss out on the fullness of His life for us. If we prioritize anything over the Lord and His word, then the supernatural, impossible life He has for us isn't available. Like that moment of pushing off a cliff, it requires abandonment. The kind of life you and I need is available only through a God who asks us to leave it all behind. This is how the Christian walk is meant to be – we are to jump in with both feet. Scripture says that a double-minded man is unstable in all his ways (see James 1:8). It's time to leave our limited, frail version of stability and comfort and live with abandonment for the One who holds us in His hands. It's time to commit and take the leap.

CHAPTER 3

Expensive Love

We would be remiss to think that we can live any kind of all in life for the Lord without the key component of who He is and what He has called us to do. We know that God is love and that His love is the strongest force in the universe. So, if we are to live a life sold out to God and live the life that He has made available for us, then it will also be a life of love. When you boil down the Scriptures to reveal the life that God calls us to, the answer, again, is love.

According to Jesus, the two greatest commandments are to love. Firstly, to love the Lord your God with all your heart, soul, mind, and strength – to love Him in a way that's all-in, with abandonment, holding nothing back. The second commandment is to share that love with people – to love our neighbor as ourselves. Jesus says that all the law and the prophets (the rest of the word of God) hang on those two commandments (see Mt. 22:40). The fullness of life that God has for us is expressed in love. Galatians 5:6 says, "the only thing that counts is faith expressing itself in love."

It doesn't get much clearer than that. That must be our takeaway; whenever we read Scripture, whenever we pray, in our attitudes and the actions we make in life – nothing matters if it's not faith expressing itself in love.

When I was a young man, my pastor, Barney Coombs, used to regularly say, "The main thing is to keep the main thing the main thing." We so easily get caught up defining all sorts of ways to live for God or serve God, but if we lose the main thing, we've missed it. Love is the main thing – and the only thing that counts is expressing our faith in love.

Galatians 2:20 says, "The life I now live in the body, I live by faith in the Son of God, who loved me and gave himself for me."

It's because of love that we are free to live the life that is described in this book. Love allows us to risk. There is always a perceived risk in love - risk that your love won't be returned, risk that you'll be rejected, risk that you'll be left vulnerable, and risk that you'll be hurt.

I remember when I was in the early days of a relationship with Elizabeth Wyns, whom I later married. We met at a youth camp when I was 18 and she was 16. For me, it was love at first sight. It took about a year for her to feel the same way, as she had just had her heart broken by a guy she liked. For her, there was a perceived risk in opening her heart to someone who might disappoint her. She liked me but wasn't sure that our long-distance relationship (we lived 3,000 miles apart) would survive. Oblivious to all this, I was falling more and more in love with this incredible young woman. I knew I loved her, but when should I actually say the words "I love you"? It's a scary thing. What if she didn't love me back? I would be putting myself out there, and I was feeling very vulnerable. But, in the end, a faint heart never won a fair maiden, and I believed that the Lord had brought us together. So, I decided to risk it and let her know (beyond the phone calls and letters and visits to see her every six months) that I loved her. I said the words for the first time. She, thankfully, replied that she loved me too, and my heart felt like it was about to explode with delight. I had found someone I wanted to love for the rest of my life. The risk paid off – and 25 years later, we remain deeply in love.

We can see this clearly played out in our earthly relationships, but do we apply the same perspective to our spiritual relationship with our Heavenly Father? Agape love (God-love) requires great cost; it is unconditional, willful, sacrificial love. It means that we do good to another at our own expense. So, if there is a cost to great love, we risk something. Cost always implies a loss of something that you possess.

As the last chapter outlined, living the life God offers us requires abandonment, leaving behind the things that seem to have value to receive something greater. Paul says, "But whatever were gains to me I now consider loss for the sake of Christ. What is more, I consider everything a loss because of the surpassing worth of knowing Christ Jesus my Lord, for whose sake I have lost all things. I consider them garbage, that I may gain Christ." Phil. 3:7-8

We must let go of everything this world considers valuable to gain all that Christ has for us. We have to die to our wants and desires so His wants and desires can manifest in our lives. As a side note, His wants and desires for you are infinitely greater than those you have for yourself. You'll find this out when you begin to live all in for Him.

One of the litmus tests for the condition of our hearts is how much we're willing to risk. Can we risk giving up things that matter so dearly? The answer is that love risks all to gain all (when we're talking about God's love). Only when we have a revelation of God's love can we turn over what is valuable and consider it garbage for the sake of knowing Christ. If we do not see God's love, we cannot make that transaction. We'll lose out to the lawyer in our heads every time. But when the love of God is realized, we gladly surrender all other claims that would offer any benefit to us.

When we realize what He is offering and the kind of life He desires us to live, we would not only accept His offer but would recognize that we'd be fools to do anything else. We are often prevented from understanding this revelation because of the distractions and other passions in our lives. We get so comfortable with what we know that we don't want to risk losing the little we have to step into the unknown. We need a revelation of the love of God to break us out of this perspective. That's why Paul says, "And I pray that you, being rooted and established in love, may have power, together with all the Lord's holy people, to grasp how wide and long and high and deep is the love of Christ, and to know this love that surpasses knowledge—that you may be filled to the measure of all the fullness of God." Eph. 3:17-18

Paul is praying that we may know just how big the love of God is. It's a love that surpasses knowledge and allows us to be filled to the measure of all the fullness of God. Without this revelation, we can't be filled with this kind of love or life.

THE IMPOSSIBLE LIFE

Let me paint a picture for you. A homeless man is pushing a shopping cart filled with cans and bottles to collect the deposit money (5 cents per can and 10 cents per bottle). Along the way, he sees a large house. He goes up the driveway and knocks on the door. A kind, well-dressed man opens the door and begins conversing with him. The homeless man asks if he has any cans or bottles to give. The man in the house says, "I do not have any of those bottles and cans, but I would like to offer you something better. I would like you to come and stay here at my house, where you will be well cared for. You'll eat at my table and wear clothes that will be provided for you every day." The kind man beckons him in and says to the man, "You don't need your shopping cart here; you can leave it outside." The homeless man stops; he thinks for a long time. He has only ever known bottles and cans as the way he could scratch out a living. Does he leave behind what he knows to embrace something different? He believes he would be safe, secure, and cared for if he went to live with the kind man, but he also knows he would lose something. He would have to live by the rules of the house, and although the man is kind, what if his rules are difficult to follow? Politely, the homeless man declines the offer and goes off to the next house seeking more bottles and cans.

This story is repeated in our lives on a regular basis. The owner of all things, the Creator of the heavens and the earth, offers us fullness of life and beckons us to come in, but we must leave behind that which we know. Are we willing to risk it? Are we willing to lose it all for His sake? If we say 'No,' then we go on without ever experiencing the benefit of the life our Lord offers us. If we say 'Yes,' we have to willingly leave behind that which doesn't belong anymore. We must dress in the clothes He provides and eat the food He prepares for us. Of course, for us who have experienced this life, our perspective isn't that we *have* to give up our lives and receive His life. Instead, we now understand that we *get* to give up our garbage compared to the riches of His grace and provisions. Our perspective must shift if we are to willingly lay down our lives. We must have a revelation of the love of God.

How much are you willing to risk? Love will put it all on the line because it is rooted and secure in the knowledge of just how big, capable, and trustworthy the God of our salvation is. That's why Jesus said with His dying words, "Father, into your hands, I commit my spirit." Luke 23:46

In both His living and His dying, Jesus gave an example of living life by laying it down. Love for God cost

Him all His heart, soul, mind, and strength. In laying down His life, He allowed us to live. You are invited into this life. He won't force it on you, but His desires for you are way beyond what you can imagine.

"Now to him who is able to do immeasurably more than all we ask or imagine, according to his power that is at work within us, to him be glory in the church and in Christ Jesus throughout all generations, for ever and ever! Amen." Eph. 3:20-21

What are you willing to risk for the one who can give you everything? He is a God of love, and if you let Him, His big love will fill every area of need and lack in your life. He desires to fill you with Himself; He desires to fill you with His expensive love.

CHAPTER 4

Beyond Belief

A couple of years ago, we took our three boys to visit Niagara Falls and Toronto in Canada. More than just seeing where their mom grew up, we wanted them to be able to experience some things up close and in person. Niagara Falls is an amazing wonder. The sheer power of the falling water, the thundering noise you can feel in your chest, and the mist that fills the air are incredible. For obvious reasons, there are guard rails beside the river and outlook area. I find I am drawn in by the speed and direction of the water. I have never had a death wish, and I was not in harm's way, but I am thankful for the railings there.

From there, we visited Toronto and went up the tallest building in Canada, the CN Tower, which stands 1,815 feet high. We took the elevator to the observation deck. As we walked around, I saw a glass floor area where you could look down at the ground (1,122 feet below). Many people would stand on the cement floor and peer over the glass to look down. But there were no guard rails around the glass floor area. In fact, many people were walking on it, enjoying the view. I realized this was tempered glass, designed to support a massive amount of weight – much like the concrete that everyone else was standing on. If the glass was designed for huge amounts of weight, then it stood to reason that my weight could certainly not affect its stability. So, I walked on the glass, and then I jumped up and down on the glass. Soon, I began stomping on the glass floor, jumping up as high as possible and then pounding my feet as hard as I could onto the glass. People were quickly leaving the area and muttering to themselves about this crazy person. But to me, it was fun; the glass was solid. I couldn't break it. I trusted in its ability to hold my weight; I believed it was secure, and I put that belief into action.

We often think that believing in something simply means understanding something to be true. But this is not how previous civilizations understood that word. In the past, the term *believe* meant to actually put your weight on it, to have faith that it will not break. You don't just think something is true; belief involves an action of trust.

One of my favorite moments in the Gospels is found in Mark chapter 9, where a father, who is at the end of his rope, comes to Jesus to see if He will heal his demon-possessed son. Verses 20-24 say, "When the spirit saw Jesus, it immediately threw the boy into a convulsion. He fell to the ground and rolled around, foaming at the mouth. Jesus asked the boy's father, 'How long has he been like this?' 'From childhood,' he answered. 'It has often thrown him into fire or water to kill him. But if you can do anything, take pity on us and help us.' 'If you can?' said Jesus. Everything is possible for one who believes.' Immediately the boy's father exclaimed, 'I do believe; help me overcome my unbelief!'"

Jesus ends up casting the demon out, but I love the father's response here. He so badly wanted to believe – but his son had been plagued with this thing for years; all he had left was a shred of belief. When Jesus offered hope that anything is possible for those who believe – the man cried out, "I do believe! Help me overcome my unbelief."

Belief and unbelief can co-exist in the same heart. How much do we believe? There's a mixture in all of us, and there are certain things that kill belief or at least limit how much faith we have. No matter how much we want to believe, we need to overcome certain things in order to have complete faith. They lower your expectations and keep you from experiencing the supernatural power of

God. I call them belief busters. They are offense, skepticism, and disappointing experiences.

The first hindrance to believing is offense. It comes when we perceive that someone has done something wrong. Perhaps they have hurt us or behaved wrongly towards someone we know and love. Our sense of injustice is triggered, and we get frustrated with them because they did not live up to our expectations. We cannot afford to be easily offended; it robs us of the supernatural power of God. We must forgive. In Mark 11:23-24, Jesus talks about moving mountains and believing that we receive what we ask for in prayer. In the very next verse, Jesus says, "And when you stand praying, if you hold anything against anyone, forgive them, so that your Father in heaven may forgive you your sins." Mark 11:25

These things are connected. Being offended will rob us of belief; we must always forgive. If we do not, Jesus makes it clear that the full power of the cross is not available to us. Nothing could be more important to living out the impossible life than this.

The second obstacle to believing is skepticism. We may find it difficult to trust people or think nothing good can happen to us. Sometimes we don't even trust that something is from God because it comes from an unexpected source.

Jesus rebuked the disciples for this. After Jesus rose from the dead, He first appeared to Mary Magdalene, who reported it to the disciples, but they didn't believe her. Then two disciples on the road to Emmaus reported seeing Jesus, but the disciples didn't believe them either. "Later Jesus appeared to the Eleven as they were eating; he rebuked them for their lack of faith and their stubborn refusal to believe those who had seen him after he had risen." Mark 16:14

Thomas wasn't the only one who doubted. Apparently, all the disciples had a hard time receiving the news from a woman who had been delivered from 7 demons and from two disciples who weren't in the inner circle. Know this about God: He loves to surprise us. Be careful not to let your expectations or preferences keep you from experiencing God's power. God might be revealing something amazing through someone you don't expect it to come from.

Finally, we must overcome the obstacle of disappointing experiences. Our experiences often don't match how we think things should be. They tell us that God doesn't always intervene. Our experiences tell us that God doesn't always heal. He doesn't always protect or provide, at least not in the way we expect Him to.

John the Baptist battled with this when he was imprisoned by King Herod. He sent his disciples to ask

Jesus, "'Are you the one who is to come, or should we expect someone else?' Jesus replied, 'Go back and report to John what you hear and see: The blind receive sight, the lame walk, those who have leprosy are cleansed, the deaf hear, the dead are raised, and the good news is proclaimed to the poor.'" Matthew 11:3-5

Jesus encouraged John and us to hold on to our belief, even when we don't see the results. We must make a choice every day. When we pray, do we expect God to move? Will we believe that what we pray for will happen this time, even after the last hundred times didn't produce anything? That's called faith. Hebrews 11:6 says, "Anyone who comes to Him (God) must believe that he exists and that he rewards those who earnestly seek him."

Do you believe that God will reward you even when you make mistakes, you sin, or fall short? The good news is that God rewards us, not because we deserve it, but because Jesus deserves it. So, when His Spirit is living in us, we can expect God to move through us. We must expect God to reward us.

You must believe God each and every time you pray. The Bible says if we don't believe, we are double-minded, and won't receive anything we pray for (see James 1:6-8). So, if we don't see it, we pray again, and we keep praying. We keep believing; we pray in faith, knowing that it's our job to pray and believe, and it's His job to move. If I live and pray in such a way that requires God to intervene, then He will.

When God asks me to do something, it often requires more than I have the capacity for. I have learned to do it anyway; I let Him perform the miracles. If I try to make the supernatural happen, it falls flat, every time. But if I can stomp on that glass floor, and blindly trust and obey, He is faithful every time. This is especially true when I've reached the end of my own abilities, my own resources, and the end of my own energy. I must learn to obey and leave the results to God.

I remember several years ago, I was speaking with the Lord and feeling restless. I was sitting around a fire pit on my back deck, pouring my heart out to God. Suddenly, I felt Him ask me a question. He said, "You're ready for a new adventure, aren't you?" Immediately my spirit leaped within me, and I said, "Yes!" I wondered what this meant. Was God going to move us somewhere new? Was He going to provide a new ministry for us? I was eager to find out.

A few weeks later, my wife was asked to return to teaching full-time in a classroom (she had retired from teaching to help raise our young children). At first, I just dismissed the idea. Of course, she can't go and work full time. We were full-time parents *and* full-time pastors. Over the next two days, God spoke to Liz about His plan for her in the classroom, and she began to get excited. Meanwhile, I got worried that this just might be God. We had a 4-year-old in pre-kindergarten and a 2-year-old and 6-month-old at home. How could I be expected to be a stay-at-home dad and a full-time pastor? Then God reminded me of His question a few weeks prior. Wait, is *this* the new adventure????

This was not what I was thinking. It was not anywhere *close* to what I thought God meant. I did not feel ready for the challenge. It was way more than my capacity. The day Liz returned to the classroom was the day her parents left for a 2-week mission trip. I was left alone with my young kids and a growing church. For the first few days, I stewed. I was in a bad mood. How could God do this to me? I was trying to write a sermon, entertain a 2-year-old, and console a crying 6-month-old. I vented to God. I said, "Lord, I'm in a bad mood." God replied, "Ok, then change it."

"Change my mood???" What kind of answer was that? Then, I remembered my father-in-law's teaching on Thanksgiving and how it was an atmosphere changer. Boy, did I ever need an atmosphere change at that moment.

So, I started giving thanks to God. First, for little things, but as I continued, it grew to greater things. Soon, I was thanking God for His calling on my life and that He was able to equip me and supply me with whatever I needed to fulfill His call. Then suddenly, the phone rang, and my good friend offered to watch the boys while I studied to preach. What used to take 12+ hours for me to prepare a sermon suddenly began to be accomplished in 2 hours. God downloaded revelation, scriptures, and more. I could barely keep up with the flow of the Holy Spirit as He took me on a journey. It continued like this for the next two years while Liz taught full-time. It became one of the best seasons of my life. I was stretched way past my comfort or qualified zone. I learned what God could do if I yielded my life. I learned that He was after more than what I could imagine or make happen on my own. He was releasing something supernatural in me.

To live the impossible life, you must do more than just believe in God. You must believe and demonstrate that Jesus is the Son of God by trusting Him with everything. The life you live, you now live by faith in Him, but none of us can do this without God's help. We need Him to change us – to increase our faith. It's ok if we are like the father in Mark 9. We can say, "We believe, Lord, but help our unbelief." If we pray this with sincerity, He will answer. He will help us, and He will increase our faith. He'll cause us to overcome offense, skepticism, and the disappointing experiences of life. He'll show Himself to be faithful and true, and He will reward us if we believe. Then, anything is possible.

CHAPTER 5

Overcoming Faith

One of the central themes of every human life is trial and obstacles. Whether through our own frailties, shortcomings, or mistakes, or those of others who influence us, the struggle is real, and it affects us at a deep level. How do we live a supernatural life when we're surrounded by battles that we can't seem to overcome? How do we keep moving when there are seasons when the hits just keep coming? None of this escapes God's awareness. It is part of His eternal plan. We have assurances from the Lord that trials will come. Jesus says, "In this world you will have trouble. But take heart! I have overcome the world." Jn. 16:33

If we dwell on this truth, it brings a level of consolation that the God of the universe is not only aware that struggles will come, but He also tells us to "take heart" because He has overcome everything that stands against us. It's difficult to hang on to that truth when the storm is raging, and we're asking God to intervene, yet He doesn't seem to answer our prayers.

When this happens, our flesh will try to take control. The flesh seeks to protect us from all kinds of threats, and when troubles surround us on every side, we move into survival mode. It is then that our enemy does his best to kick us when we're down. He fills our minds with analyzing why and how we find ourselves here. We go through a period of self-examination. Perhaps God is punishing us for some specific sin or failure. We know God is patient, but we also know that our own hearts and flesh are hopelessly corrupt, and they begin to condemn us. We have feelings of guilt and failure as we review our shortcomings. This usually turns into self-pity as we try to cope with our unpleasant reality. This often leads to anger and blaming others for their perceived part in our failures. Even God gets blamed for our bad situation. After all, He could have kept all these bad things from happening.

This causes a downward spiral of thoughts and emotions that are standard procedure for our enemy, who is laser-focused on attacking us. It's not just our body, relationships, or mental state he is out to destroy. Those are secondary targets. His real goal is to take out the one thing that will will allow us to overcome. His target is to destroy our faith. This is what your life is all about.

Every battle you fight has to do with your faith. It's not so much the things around you that are the obstacle; it is the assault on your faith that you must defend against. Your enemy knows that if he can shoot down your faith and keep you stuck in a loop of failure, guilt, self-pity, and anger, you'll never fly again. You'll be walking along the path of this life wounded, not able to overcome, and not moving into who God made you to be.

The best way to fight for your faith is by reminding your heart and mind of what God has said. After all, faith comes by hearing and hearing by the word of God. So, we should memorize and retrain our minds to go back to God's word when we're in a battle. It is our sword with which we can strike down the enemy and his deceptive thoughts. There are so many uplifting and reassuring verses we can use.

Romans 5:20 says, "Where sin increased, grace increased all the more."

Hebrews 13:5 reinforces God's promise to never leave or forsake us.

The story in 2 Chronicles chapter 20 outlines the overwhelming odds faced by King Jehoshaphat. God's word comes to His people in verse 15, saying, "Do not be afraid or discouraged . . . For the battle is not yours, but God's."

1 John 4:4 says, "You, dear children, are from God and have overcome them because the one who is in you is greater than the one who is in the world."

These are tools that we use for our fight; our ability to overcome depends on them. There's bad news all around, but that doesn't mean it's the truth. There is a bigger perspective, a greater reality than what we see. Like the servant of Elisha who could only see the advancing army, we need our eyes opened to the spiritual reality we dwell in. In 2 Kings 6:16-17, it records the words of Elisha. He says to his servant, "'Don't be afraid . . . Those who are with us are more than those who are with them.' And Elisha prayed, 'Open his eyes, Lord, so that he may see.' Then the Lord opened the servant's eyes, and he looked and saw the hills full of horses and chariots of fire all around Elisha."

It's precisely in the moment when we feel under siege that God is able to open our eyes to see a greater reality.

Paul tells us to fight the good fight of faith. We must be wise to the enemy's tactics and not let him steal our faith from right under our noses. The battle is not with our circumstances or the people around us; it is the fight of faith. Faith is like the spiritual oxygen we need to survive. If someone is cutting off your air supply, your body instinctively fights for breath. So, when the enemy comes to cut off your faith, don't let him. Fight back! But we must recognize it as the enemy and not as our own thoughts. How easy it is for our minds to be filled with doubt. "Did God really say that?" "Why does God let this happen to you?" "Look how others are blessed and you are not." These are lies – lies to steal your faith.

It's in the storm and deluge when you need to carry an extra supply of faith. It's like an oxygen tank so that you can breathe when you are out of air. If you are running low, borrow some from your fellow believers because this faith is something we are called to both give and receive. Hanging around people of faith is a lifeline. When I need faith, I talk to someone in the Lord who has the gift of faith, and I breathe it in. In time, I learn to get my own tank so that I'm not running out so often. We keep filling the tank with His word and His promises.

We need one another in this fight, but don't think you need to have it all figured out first before you help others. Sometimes, God gives to us only as we give out. I've found that it's much easier to have faith for other people than for myself. So, start by blessing others with faith. Many Christians are so entrenched in their own battle to overcome that they miss out on the blessing of giving faith to others. The most valuable thing you can give someone is faith. Push them back into God; pray a prayer of faith. If you don't know where to start or how to do this, start by proclaiming scripture. It's full of the promises of God that are the basis and foundation of our faith. They will build your faith as you speak them out.

In time, we realize that the obstacles and challenges of life are a gift. They are the greenhouse in which faith grows. Faith can grow and form when we can't see any way through. After all, we walk by faith and not by sight. How hopeless it is to walk around without faith or sight. But when the lights go out, and you can't see where you're going, you put your trust in God; that's when faith is born.

Nobody said the journey was going to be easy, and if they did, they were either lying or hopelessly ill-informed. When hard times come, we have to recognize that our flesh has one goal – to remove ourselves from any unpleasant situation as quickly as possible. This, however, shortcuts the process by which our overcoming faith can grow.

Faith is the only means by which I can become an overcomer in this life. "For everyone born of God overcomes the world. This is the victory that has overcome the world, even our faith. Who is it that overcomes the world? Only the one who believes that Jesus is the Son of God." 1 John 5:4-5

The truth is that God is big, powerful, and loving enough to use what the enemy intends for evil in our lives. He turns it into something for our good.

Judges 3:1-2 says, "These are the nations the Lord left to test all those Israelites who had not experienced any of the wars in Canaan (he did this only to teach warfare to the descendants of the Israelites who had not had previous battle experience)."

But wait. Didn't God tell the Israelites to take possession of the Promised Land and to drive out every nation? So, the only reason there are still enemies in their land is because of their failure to obey God. Fast forward some years, and God, in His infinite wisdom, uses Israel's failure and turns it into a tool for overcoming. Isn't that what it says? The Lord left these nations to help teach warfare to a new generation. God was going to teach them how to fight – and this was a much more valuable gift than if God had granted them peace with their enemies, who would one day become a snare to them. God was stirring something up in them, teaching them how to trust in Him again and how to rely on His strength for future battles that He knew would come.

I have found this to be true in my own life. Although I don't enjoy the process, God has taken the hard times in my life (brought on either by my own failure or just because I live in a fallen, broken world), to teach me and grow my faith. It was the hard times that taught me how to have faith. In each of these moments, I wasn't asking for faith; I was asking for help. But I've come to realize that God's ways are much higher than my ways. He knows what I'm going to need on my journey. He knows that faith will end up being a much greater gift than whatever else I was asking for because it gives me the power to overcome any trial, not just one specific problem.

After years of first-hand experience with this, the focus of my prayer life has changed. Now, instead of praying, "God, please change this circumstance," I am beginning to understand that God may choose to leave the circumstance unchanged because what He wants to change is me. The Father wants Christ to be formed in me; He wants to change me into the image of His beloved Son. He wants to fill me with His power and make me an overcomer! How is He going to do that if all He ever does is blast obstacles out of the way for me? Instead, He will often make me wait, and learn how to deal with the enemy. He wants to teach me to be an overcomer.

Romans 8:28 says, "And we know that in all things God works for the good of those who love him, who have been called according to his purpose."

Do you know this to be true in your life? You need to believe and know it for yourself if you're going to become an overcomer. If we trust Him in times of battles and pain, He will give us the gift of faith, and that will open the door to God's supernatural power to be released. God will do the impossible and turn death into life. In the next chapter, we will take a closer look at this.

CHAPTER 6

Death of a Seed

I'm up to bat, and the bases are loaded in the bottom of the ninth inning. My team is down by 3 runs, and there are 2 outs. The count is full, at 3 balls and 2 strikes. The crowd is buzzing with anticipation. Everything is riding on this next pitch. The pitcher winds into his motion and delivers a fastball down the middle of the plate. I swing my bat and . . .

Baseball was a childhood dream of mine. I played for five years on different teams and rehearsed the above scenario in my backyard a thousand times in my head. Of course, in my imagination, I would always crank a high, towering grand slam home run out of the park while the crowd went wild (I would even make the sound of the roaring crowd with the breath of my mouth) as I rounded the bases and jumped into the arms of my adoring teammates. Of course, it was usually just me in the backyard alone, but the dream was very much alive.

I was actually pretty good. I played shortstop; I had great range and could make almost any throw with accuracy. I was a fine hitter as well and could get on base most of the time. At age 12, I went to a special baseball camp put on by one of the Houston Astros' players in my small hometown. We were in awe to be with a real professional athlete. I was one of about 20 kids at the camp. We played 6-out innings, so the MLB star could spend more time analyzing the kids in the field. I was at my usual shortstop position and made five of the six outs that inning. The major league player was impressed and told me that I was well on my way to having a big future in baseball. The dream became even more alive.

The next season, my friend and I were accidentally registered in the wrong league. We were 12 years old and small for our age, but we were registered in the 13 to 16-year-old league. Suddenly, it was like boys playing against men. The first curve ball I faced as a batter, I dove onto my back, thinking it was about to hit me. The ball proceeded to curve right over the middle of the plate. The umpire looked at me lying on the ground and said, "Strike." "Oh boy," I thought, "I'm in big trouble." That season, I only managed one hit, but my fielding was still good. After the season, I spent a few weeks in the batting cage, working on my hitting. I knew I would improve and keep the dream alive if I kept practicing.

But then God spoke.

I knew what His voice sounded like in my heart. He told me He wanted me to give up baseball. What? How could I give up on my dream? It was only a year ago I was being praised by a professional player. I couldn't possibly give up now. I knew, however, that if I really trusted God, I would have to follow through, so I quit – never to return to the game I loved for so long.

Why do I tell you this story? Do I have any regrets? Not one bit. My life has taken me on such an adventure in the Lord; I wouldn't trade it for the world. There's a spiritual truth contained in the death of a dream that we need to lay hold of. Listen to the words of Jesus:

"Very truly I tell you, unless a kernel of wheat falls to the ground and dies, it remains only a single seed. But if it dies, it produces many seeds. Anyone who loves their life will lose it, while anyone who hates their life in this world will keep it for eternal life." John 12:24-25

Jesus laid down His life as a seed planted in the ground. His sacrifice produced the seeds of life for you and me. When we live an impossible life, we produce more than what is possible in the natural. God gives us the picture of a seed that must die in order to produce fruit. This truth must be applied to each of our lives. If we are really seeking to live a life of supernatural power, then we will have to die to some of our dreams – even ones we feel that God has given us.

This leads into a greater truth; God allows suffering in our lives to produce something beautiful. Just like the seed that needs to die in order to become fruitful, Jesus led the way and showed us that His mission was incomplete without the process of death working in Him.

Scripture says, "In bringing many sons and daughters to glory, it was fitting that God, for whom and through whom everything exists, should make the pioneer of their salvation perfect through what he suffered." Heb 2:10

That's an interesting choice of words, "It was fitting." In other words, suffering isn't just what happens as a punishment; it is part of God's design for this life. While we are guaranteed that in the life to come, there will be no more sorrow and no more pain, we are equally guaranteed that in this life, we must endure suffering. That is part of the process of Christ being formed in us. It was fitting for the pioneer of our salvation to be made perfect (or complete) through suffering because it's also the process by which we are made perfect and complete. There is something in the plan of God by which He makes

Himself known, more present, and real in the moments of suffering. Not only that, but if we join in the fellowship of Christ's sufferings, we shall also join Him in His glory (see Romans 8:17).

It is up to us to either yield to the process of death working in us, or to refuse to partake in that process. If we refuse, then our access to an impossible life is closed. This is the path God has chosen to release His supernatural power and life. We like to hear devotionals, tweets, and sermons that talk about blessings, and they are true, but not many of us like to hear words about the suffering that is required. This, however, is necessary to release the true life of God in us. It's not a popular teaching but an essential one. It is a path of life that is required but rarely appreciated.

When my wife, Liz, and I were first married, we often talked about having children. We loved kids and couldn't wait to be parents. We were young when we got married, 21 and 19 years old. After a year or two, we decided to try to have kids. Months went by, and then years. We finally consulted a doctor, who, after running some tests, told us that we would not be able to have children.

We were devastated; we couldn't believe it. His words were like a gut punch that took the air out of us. My flesh immediately began wrestling with God. How could He deny us such a good thing? This was a dream that He had put in both of our hearts. As an aside, God is ok with us being real and honest with Him. He desires an intimate relationship with us, and He can handle our venting to Him. King David, in many of his Psalms, didn't shy away from asking God hard questions about the seeming injustice of life. After every complaint, however, he turned back to praise and put his trust in God again.

This is an essential lesson for us. God is who He says He is. He is good, He is able, trustworthy, and faithful, and He is love. Despite the circumstances that surround us, part of our faith journey should end up with us acknowledging who He is in the middle of conflicting evidence.

Despite the words of doctors, we trusted God and continued to pray. After a couple of years, Liz got pregnant. We were overjoyed! We just knew God wouldn't let us down. Suddenly, at ten weeks, Liz miscarried, and we lost the baby. I spiraled into anger toward God. How could He allow this to happen? I found myself feeling distant from Him and began walking in the flesh more and more. God worked in my life over the next while and brought me to repentance and a renewed relationship with Him.

About three months later, Liz got pregnant again. We told the whole church as soon as we found out. Some people said we were brave to do so, implying that people don't tell others until after the first trimester just in case they miscarry. But we wanted all the support we could get. At the 10-week mark, we had a checkup, and the nurse couldn't find a heartbeat. We held onto hope that God was the author of life and could work a miracle. We stood on God's word and asked the church to pray. A week later, Liz miscarried again. This time, instead of anger and disillusionment, I found that there was grace for us in the moment. We felt sad but not devastated. We knew God was working; we could feel the prayers of the church holding us up, and God comforted us in a very real way. Even while we were at the hospital while Liz was miscarrying, the staff in the ER kept coming in to check on us. This isn't unusual, but they would stay for lengthy periods just talking. The primary doctor hovered in our room for a long time before finally asking if she could just hang out with us. She said that she couldn't believe the peace that had filled our room, and she just wanted to remain in it. God had released something supernatural through our suffering.

Afterward, because we were so open with our journey, several ladies came up to Liz and told her that they had suffered through miscarriages alone, feeling shame and disappointment, and hadn't told a soul. So, through our yielding to God, He comforted us and used us to minister healing to many others.

Fast forward another year, and we moved to the United States from Canada. Liz got pregnant again. This time, she was extremely sick with morning sickness, which wasn't the case for the first two pregnancies. We celebrated each time she threw up, knowing her body was still pregnant. She carried the baby full term, and Ethan, our oldest son, was born. It was a miracle. The doctors still told us after we had him that we wouldn't be able to have any more children. We now have three sons – all miracles. It happened as a result of a seed and a dream that had died and then produced many seeds.

Romans 5:3-5 says, "We also glory in our sufferings, because we know that suffering produces perseverance; perseverance, character; and character, hope. And hope does not put us to shame."

The process of suffering is so important; it releases God's life in us. As we continue to trust God, He produces all kinds of supernatural blessings that we can't summon on our own. Some of the blessings are godly perseverance, character, and hope. It becomes a path by which God is glorified because He takes that which is dead and brings it back to life. When we yield our heart's desires to God, He is able to keep what we commit to

Him. He loves us more than we love ourselves. He knows what's best for us. He is good and He is faithful. If we delight ourselves in Him, He promises to give us the desires of our hearts. That is because our hearts will be set on the things of the Lord. When we receive what's on God's heart, we receive great purpose and joy.

If you are going through a hard season, know this: God will be there in the middle of your suffering. He will comfort and bless you as He works on your heart and brings you into His supernatural life.

CHAPTER 7

It's About Time

They say timing is everything; it's hard to disagree. As an avid sports fan, I have lived the agony and ecstasy of the games of inches and milliseconds. Olympic gold medal winners and world record holders can often be determined by one hundredth of a second. Timing is also important in our relationships; whether with our spouse or children, there is a good time to bring up something challenging, and there is definitely a wrong time to bring up difficult matters. For example, when you're already in the middle of a relational conflict, it is not the right time to bring up a myriad of other issues or grievances that you feel need to be addressed. This is also true in the business world. When investing in the stock market or buying and selling property, timing plays a huge part in whether these endeavors succeed or fail.

We serve a God who functions outside of time, and it's a very good thing that we do. It allows us to have the confidence that our times are in His hands, that He sees the beginning from the end and is able to lead us forward. The problem is our perspective. Dealing with a God who doesn't have our restrictions is a blessing on the one hand, but on the flip side, it can lead to our frustration. We eventually, however, learn that His ways are not our ways, His thoughts are not our thoughts, and His timing is definitely not our timing. Jesus closes the book of Revelation by saying to John, "See, I am coming soon." That was spoken almost 2,000 years ago. Clearly, God has a different definition of 'soon' than most of us. However, Scripture assures us that *our* perspective is the fallible one.

"The Lord is not slow in keeping his promise, as some understand slowness. Instead he is patient with you, not wanting anyone to perish, but everyone to come to repentance." 2 Peter 3:9

In other words, we don't know what in the world is going on, but He does, and He is working out His plan to perfection; He won't be rushed, and that's a good thing. If He were prone to be rushed, then you and I would miss out on the redemptive mercy of God. Instead, because He's patient, He works out repentance, salvation, and restoration for those who call on His name.

Paul tells us that we all see and know through an imperfect lens. "For now we see only a reflection as in a mirror; then we shall see face to face. Now I know in part; then I shall know fully, even as I am fully known." 1 Cor. 13:12

We often fail to see God's sovereign understanding of time. Here again, is where the impossible life can be missed or realized. We must trust God and hold onto His promises during times of drought, pain, and especially during times of waiting. Patience is required. Patience isn't just choosing to pause everything in life and dig your heels in until you get the answer you need. Life goes on, and we wait.

I learned a lesson about waiting on the Lord while I was in my senior year of high school. I knew I was called into the ministry but wasn't sure what path I was going to take. I narrowed it down to two options: Go off to Bible College in England, or stay at home in Vancouver to help lead the youth group. I began seeking the Lord starting in September, knowing that I would have to make a decision by the spring regarding which direction I would take. I like to plan ahead, so I gave God plenty of time to answer my question. That way, I wouldn't be rushed at the end. However, God would not answer my question. I prayed and prayed and asked God for a word, a dream, a confirmation of some sort as to the direction I was to take. Nothing.

It was like God was intentionally avoiding me on the topic. He would speak to me about all sorts of other things, so it wasn't like I was out of step with hearing Him. He just wouldn't give me clarity regarding this decision. Finally, it was the month of May. I had to decide in the next couple of weeks. I was frustrated. I said, "God, I gave you nine months to speak to me, and you *still* haven't given me direction. I just want to do Your will. I don't want to make a mistake. I don't want to move until I hear you."

I found myself at a Christian youth night when in the middle of the worship time, a prophet stood up and shared a word that the Lord had given him. He said, "There's someone here looking for road signs." My ears perked up. That was me. The prophet continued, "But you're looking for road signs while you're parked in the garage. God says to back out of the driveway and start driving, and then you'll see the road signs." I took it as the word of the Lord to me. I said, "Ok, Lord, I hear you. I will start moving. I think you want me to go to Bible College in England." Immediately, I heard the voice of the Lord tell me, "No, you need to stay here and help with the youth." I couldn't believe it. All that time, I was waiting on the Lord, and really, He was waiting on me.

It taught me a valuable lesson about how God treats His children. He's not just waiting for us to make a mistake and then punish us for picking wrong. He's willing to lead and guide us, but He desires for us to actively wait. That means keep moving, keep growing, and keep listening, even when you feel stuck. An active posture of trusting in the Lord is required as we wait on Him. This releases the supernatural; as you step forward, He adjusts your steps if you are paying attention.

Hebrews 10:35-36 puts it this way, "So do not throw away your confidence; it will be richly rewarded. You need to persevere so that when you have done the will of God, you will receive what he has promised."

We need to persevere in trusting that the Lord knows how to lead us and that He will be faithful to His word.

Ecclesiastes 11:1 says to cast your bread upon the waters, and after many days you will find it again.

Note the word *many*. After *many* days you will find it again. God is not shy to let us know that sometimes when we wait on Him, it takes a minute; an hour; a week; a year; a decade; a lifetime. God, where *are* You? He is looking for our active partnership with Him. Sometimes we have to wait because of other people's issues or the judgments that come to our fallen world.

Caleb and Joshua were 2 out of 12 spies who were sent to investigate the Promised Land. They were the only ones who had faith. The other ten only saw the challenges, and they filled the people with fear. As a result of the nation's disobedience, not Caleb and Joshua's, they had to wander in the wilderness for 40 years. Caleb and Joshua were the only ones from that generation who inherited what God had promised. I'm sure it was difficult, but they waited on the Lord.

After 40 years, they entered the Promised Land, and Caleb said, "So here I am today, eighty-five years old! I am still as strong today as the day Moses sent me out; I'm just as vigorous to go out to battle now as I was then. Now give me this hill country that the Lord promised me that day." Joshua 14:10-12

He was still strong. This was supernatural. An 85-year-old shouldn't be able to have the vigor of a young man. Caleb made good on his desire, conquering the land and taking possession of his inheritance, but it took patience and waiting for the timing of the Lord.

What about you? How long have you been waiting for the promises of God to be fulfilled? Perhaps you are waiting for children, or a promotion; maybe you have been waiting for healing or a word from God; many are waiting for a breakthrough. At these times, we cry out like the Psalmist, "How long, O Lord?"

The word of God speaks right to these life situations. "But as for you, be strong and do not give up, for your work will be rewarded." 2 Chron. 15:7

The promise doesn't come without a challenge, and that is by design. If we could inherit the promises of God through our own effort, we would attribute some or all of our success to our own ability. So, God, in His wisdom, makes it beyond the reach of our natural intellect and strength so that He may release something supernatural.

Hebrews 11:6 says, ". . . anyone who comes to him must believe that he exists and that he rewards those who earnestly seek him."

Do you believe that God will reward you? How long will you hold on to that belief? In the face of what dangers or length of time or impossible circumstances will you be willing to still trust the Lord and believe that His word will come to pass? We can easily grow anxious during uncomfortable waiting times.

Scripture says, "Let your gentleness be evident to all. The Lord is near. Do not be anxious about anything, but in every situation, by prayer and petition, with thanksgiving, present your requests to God. And the peace of

God, which transcends all understanding, will guard your hearts and your minds in Christ Jesus." Phil. 4:5-7

In the face of contrary circumstances, we are called to experience and know that which goes beyond knowledge, that which transcends understanding. It's supernatural; it's beyond what is possible for man.

If we don't respond in faith, then the impossible is unavailable. The opposite of faith is fear. It's only normal to get weary, but we serve a God who is above the normal. We have the word, Spirit, and people of God with us to strengthen us along the way. Even Moses needed Aaron and Hur to hold his arms up during the battle.

We are called to embrace the process, and instead of throwing our arms down with exhaustion, we need to throw ourselves into the supernatural provision of God and lay hold of His promises through faith. This is about knowing something that is unknowable. It's something that only comes by faith. In order to be active in the impossible, we must use the power of our words through our confession of faith. Practically, we must stop giving voice to our fears and anxieties and start giving voice to our faith. How often do we verbalize what we don't like? We complain when things go wrong. Instead, we need to verbalize our dependence and trust in Almighty God, who "gives life to the dead and calls into being things that were not." Rom. 4:17

If we put our trust in Him and give voice to our faith instead of our fears, it would change our world. That's when *peace* comes (see Phil. 4:6-7); when we refuse to be anxious and instead, we say something to God about it without complaining. We present our requests to God with *thanksgiving*. We give thanks because we know the end of the story. We give thanks because we know He loves us. We give thanks because there is a supply of grace for us to walk through each day that allows us to do more than just survive; we become overcomers. We thank God because there's a truth far greater than our circumstances.

Scripture encourages us to consider Jesus and press on. It says, "fixing our eyes on Jesus, the pioneer, and perfecter of faith. For the joy set before him, he endured the cross, scorning its shame, and sat down at the right hand of the throne of God. Consider him who endured such opposition from sinners, so that you will not grow weary and lose heart." Heb. 12:2-3

Beyond the encouragement of Christ's example, we also have a promise from the Lord. We read, "Let us not become weary in doing good, for at the proper time we will reap a harvest if we do not give up." Gal. 6:9

The promises of the Lord are all about timing. There's no lack in God's world, no place where He cannot fulfill His will. It requires only trust and perseverance to hold onto the truth of God's word. He never fails. If we hold on, we will not fail either. Despite the challenges we face, the truth is that He has overcome; He is the author and finisher of our faith. So don't grow weary. Wait on the Lord, and He will renew your strength. Allow Him to work patience in your life and activate the faith He's given. You will receive supernatural power from on high to run and not grow weary, to walk and not faint, and even to soar on the wings of eagles (see Isa 40:31). Only an impossible-working God can turn our weakness and our waiting into strength. Then, He will release His supernatural life.

CHAPTER 8

The Heart of the Matter

I was sitting in the doctor's waiting room, surrounded by people twice my age. I was 37 and waiting to see a cardiologist, hoping to get some answers. It didn't make any sense. My family had no history of heart disease, and my symptoms came out of the blue. After examining me and taking tests, the doctor could only give an educated guess as to what was wrong with me. Pericarditis was to blame, so they said. It was causing the pain I had been feeling in my heart, and the corresponding weakness in my body.

It started several weeks earlier. I had recently returned from a mission trip to Haiti and was driving to visit a friend when suddenly, I felt pain surround my heart, and a squeezing pressure that shot up to my ear. It almost took my breath away. I managed to stay on the road and made it to my friend's house. Uncertain of what was happening, I didn't stay long. I drove home and reported the symptoms to my wife. The sensation of pressure wouldn't leave. I thought maybe I had strained a muscle. After a few days, we consulted with a church friend of ours who was an ER nurse. She asked if it felt like an elephant was sitting on my chest, which is often a sign of a heart attack. I replied that it felt more like a warthog than an elephant and proceeded to describe the initial incident to her. She recommended that we see the doctor right away.

After a series of EKG scans at a clinic, I was sent immediately to the hospital, where I was monitored and examined. They didn't think it was a heart attack but weren't sure what it was, so they made an appointment with the cardiologist.

Having a name for the condition seemed to help ease my mind a little bit. After all, anything wrong with the heart feels pretty scary. Pericarditis is the inflammation of the heart sack, and while it is sometimes mild, it can be a chronic condition that never goes away. I was suffering. I had begun to lose all my strength. It got to the point where I couldn't pick up my kids or exert myself physically without having a fever spike, and I would have to take a 2-hour nap. It went on for a long time. Days turned into weeks, and weeks dragged into months. I couldn't function in any sort of normal life. I am a doer. I love to live life fast, but suddenly, I was on the couch, unable to help around the house, play with my kids, or even go to the church I was pastoring.

To make matters worse, our church congregation had just moved into this massive building, which required so much work, and I was heavily involved. I was the main person in charge of leading the effort to help restore the building. I couldn't understand why God would allow this. If ever there was a time when I needed to be functional, it was now – we were in a massive new building, I was pastoring a growing church, and raising three young boys. This was simply the worst time to be sidelined with sickness. Surely God needed me; I was the man for this task, but now I was left lying on the couch.

Sitting and doing nothing are among my least favorite things. It was as if God was stripping away who I was, and there was no relief in sight. I prayed as much as I could and repented of everything I could think of. I tried a host of different medical and homeopathic remedies. Nothing worked. I was taking 800mg of ibuprofen pills every 4 hours just to take the edge off the pain.

Then, near Christmas time, the pain started to subside a little bit. It was enough for me to go to church and participate. As a worship leader, I would lead with an acoustic guitar most weeks, and only near Christmas, when the reprieve came, was I strong enough to do this again. That's when I observed something interesting. My shoulder and heart area were so sore I couldn't bear the weight of the guitar strap without inflicting debilitating pain. This happened when I practiced at home, but as soon as I was on stage at the church building and playing for worship, the pain would be gone. After worship, I would return to my seat for the rest of the service, and the pain would return. I began to realize that this was just as much a spiritual attack as a physical one. I sought the Lord, asking how to fight this spiritual battle. My symptoms had not changed except when I was leading worship. So, I led worship as often as I could to get a bit of relief. This reprieve was a much-needed gift.

I had been seeking a word from the Lord and a breakthrough for so long; I knew I couldn't give up. I had to keep fighting, even if it was only for my family and the church. Then, one Sunday morning, it happened. I woke up and felt the Lord tell me, "It is done." I felt different in spirit, but not in body. I tried to stir up my faith, so I thought maybe I should skip the painkillers and just see if it was true. Then, just before we left the house for church, I caved in and took my regular allotment of ibuprofen, just in case I had heard God wrong (Oh, me of little faith). I am so thankful that God is gracious. While leading worship that morning, the Lord released healing in the congregation. Many people came up to the front for healing.

I continued to lead worship as people were being healed. It was during that time that a prophet in our church came to the front and just stared at me. I closed my eyes to worship but then would open them every few seconds. Each time I checked, he was still looking at me with laser-sharp focus. To be honest, I felt a little awkward. After the service, he came up to me and told me that the Lord had shown him a spot in my back that was being healed. He put his finger right on a massive area of inflammation on my back. I had told no one that my back was in pain. All anyone knew was that my heart was hurting. When he did this, I knew it was a confirmation of what God had said to me earlier in the morning, "It is done." That evening, during our weekly youth group gathering, I told the young people what had happened. I was going to put it into practice and declare my testimony. I told them I would no longer take any pills for the pain but would take God at His word. I was willing to be the faith guinea pig to see if what I thought God had said would come to pass.

I went off my painkillers and began to live as though I was healed. Although the pain did not immediately go away, my strength returned. I could now function and push through the pain without the debilitating weakness. I took this as a sign that I was healed and needed to live it out. Then, one morning, God gave me a verse from Jeremiah 17:14. It said, "Heal me, Lord, and I will be healed; save me and I will be saved." It leaped off the page at me. It was the word of the Lord for me. Right there, in that moment, I took authority and commanded my heart to obey the word of the Lord. I said, "Heart, the word of God says you are healed, so come into alignment with the word of the Lord. You are healed." Immediately the pain shrunk back and disappeared. You should have seen my face. It was like a kid who had just discovered a hidden treasure chest. I honestly had never experienced anything like that before. It was an instantaneous response to God's word. I had seen it in others but never in myself.

Several hours later, the pain began to return, and I repeated this proclamation. Immediately, the pain went away. I was starting to activate my healing. The word of God had the power to do what my desperate prayers had been unable to do for six months. I was ecstatic. God had given me a new weapon. The path of healing continued for several weeks, and God made me more and more bold in declaring His victory through His word. Eventually, the pain stopped completely. God had made me an overcomer. I was living in victory.

After about a year of living pain-free, I was hit again. Out of the blue, I felt the same heart pain. I pulled out my trusty old verse and proclamation, and with full confidence, I spoke forth the word of God. This time, the pain didn't budge. I tried it again, but still nothing happened. I felt weak, like I needed to lie down and rest. I was filled with an overwhelming feeling that I couldn't overcome. Suddenly, I felt something inside of me tell me not to take this lying down. I needed to persevere and fight. I paced the floor and prayed as fervently as I could. Just then, the Scripture came to mind where Jesus said, "Get behind me, Satan; you do not have in mind the things of God, but the things of man." Mt. 16:23

So, I spoke it out loud, and in an instant, the pain shriveled up and disappeared. I was so excited. Now I had *two* weapons in my toolbelt to use against the enemy.

God used this whole ordeal to turn me into a fighter. My faith grew so much, and God taught me how to overcome. It's not just in matters of my physical health that I now fight. God put a rod of steel in me that now gets emboldened whenever the enemy attacks. It has changed my life. I ask myself, "Did God really have to inflict six months of debilitating pain and weakness on me?" My answer is, "Yes, He probably did."

He knew that I wouldn't become who He wanted me to be without this incredible journey. I am a different man, and so thankful for that chapter in my journey. I'm not just thankful that it is over; although I am glad to be pain-free, I am also thankful for the journey. It made me who I am today. It brought me closer to God. He revealed Himself as the strength of my life, and He glorified His name in the process.

Asaph wrote these words, "Whom have I in heaven but you? And earth has nothing I desire besides you. My flesh and my heart may fail, but God is the strength of my heart and my portion forever." Psalm 73:25-26

God is after our hearts. It's easy to give God things that are not so central to who we are. We can give Him our time, service, worship, money, and in my case, even a lifetime of working in the church, but it is never enough. If it's not the deepest part of who we are, then we retain some measure of being in control. When God strips away all that we are, as He did with Job, we find out where our heart is. He's looking for a complete response. It took me a long time to learn the lessons He had for me, and I am still learning, but with all my heart, I can now say, "You can have it all, Lord."

CHAPTER 9

Fruitfulness

As previously mentioned, I grew up in the Okanagan Valley in beautiful British Columbia. One of the blessings of this beautiful part of the world is the abundance of fruit. There are apple orchards, cherry trees, apricot and plum trees, grape vineyards, and much more. My family had apricot trees and a McIntosh apple tree in our yard. I loved watching the green apples blush red as the cooler nights set in during September. Before long, apples were everywhere. Dozens upon dozens of crispy, perfectly flavored apples. It meant more than just apples to munch on; it meant apple sauce, apple pies, apple turnovers, and my favorite, apple juice. I loved taking the apples to the apple press and watching them squeeze the rich, dark brown, pure apple juice from them. Many people would dilute the concentrated juice for their own personal consumption, but I loved to drink it in full strength, poured straight from the green glass bottles in our pantry.

When we moved to South Carolina, we got to experience new kinds of vegetation, palm trees being among them. We were struck with the landscape when we first visited the Carolinas. It was so green, covered in trees and a variety of beautiful vegetation. It's a different story, however, when it comes to growing grass. In Canada, we hardly gave any notice to the grass, except that we had to mow it weekly. We didn't have to plant it or seed it; we rarely had to water it. It just grew. In the South, I have been engaged in what I like to call "turf wars." Getting grass to grow has ended up being a decades-long battle. It's a constant fight against the heat, battled with copious amounts of expensive watering. Every spring, I have to pull up the crabgrass and add pre-emergent to kill any other weeds or unwanted grass types. This is followed by a process of overseeding the ground and covering the newly seeded bare patches with soil and peat moss so the birds don't eat the seed. Fertilizer is also necessary to get the best chance at a fuller, more heat-resistant lawn. I must repeat this process in the fall, along with aerating the soil. If I do all of this, I just might be able to get it to grow and earn the right to mow it weekly for 4-5 months— what a battle!

Fruitfulness can be a battle. Despite all the work I put into it, I am powerless to do anything that will actually cause the seeds to grow. The truth is, the farmer can no more make the seeds grow than cause the sun to shine. Yet, he plays an integral role in providing the right environment for growth and life. Jesus talked about this in the parable of the sower. The main point of the parable is not so much about the sower, but rather the soil. If the soil is right, then the seed is fruitful, and it multiplies 30, 60, and even 100 times what was sown. This is what the Christian life is supposed to be like. God's word, the seed, is meant to bear supernatural, exponential fruit in our lives. It is our job to partner with God in creating the conditions for fruitfulness in the soil of our hearts.

He is the master farmer. He works to till the soil of our hearts to make it receptive to life and growth. If the seed is the word of God, and the word of God, according to Isaiah 55:10-11, always accomplishes that for which it was sent, so that there is seed for the Sower and bread for the eater, then the issue of fruitfulness is never a result of bad seed. The issue of fruitfulness depends upon time, suitable growing conditions, and good soil. It takes a process of turning over our lives, revealing the rocky areas, pulling out thorns, and re-making the rough path, so it's suitable for growth. It involves a process of refining and pruning before the fruit is ready.

Jesus told us that His life was pruned by His Heavenly Father. Even the fruitful things in Jesus' life were pruned, so He could bear more fruit (see John 15:1-2). God is after more fruit in our lives as well. We are branches of the vine, and I have noticed that we cannot tell the difference between cutting off and pruning. As far as the branch is concerned, it is just getting cut. We feel the work of God in our lives as He cuts away the dead branches and prunes back the fruitful things. Only God knows how to do this perfectly. We tend to believe that we can be an active participant in helping God prune others. We can see their flaws and blind spots. It's so easy to point out where others need to change, but when it comes to our own lives, it is so personal we usually can't see the forest for the trees. We can't see the bigness of God's plan. All we know is what we experience, which according to Jesus' words in John 15, will involve cutting.

If we allow God to work with us, He will reveal the secrets of the Kingdom of Heaven, which run contrary to how we think things should function. In the natural world, it's survival of the fittest. In God's world, His power is made perfect in weakness (see 2 Cor. 12:9).

Paul builds on this revelation, telling us that this is actually God's method. "But God chose the foolish things of the world to shame the wise; God chose the weak things of the world to shame the strong. God chose the lowly things of this world and the despised things—and the things that are not—to nullify the things that are." 1 Cor. 1:27-28

This is part of His plan. He doesn't pick the strongest to do the greatest things. He chooses the lowly. He lifts up the needy. He fills the hungry with good things, and so the supernatural power of God is displayed. Out of poverty, He releases abundance. This is God's plan for fruitfulness. The secret to fruitfulness is trusting God in our lack.

Let's take a closer look at this through the object lesson of the miraculous feeding of the 5,000. Matthew 14 and Mark chapter 6 set the scene for us. I encourage you to go and read through it for yourself and see how God unfolds this truth.

First, we learn about the death of John the Baptist at the hands of King Herod. "John's disciples came and took his body and buried it. Then they went away and told Jesus. When Jesus heard what had happened, he withdrew by boat privately to a solitary place. Hearing of this, the crowds followed him on foot from the towns." Mt. 14:12-13

Matthew indicates that Jesus wanted to get away with His disciples because of the grief of losing His cousin. Now, let's look at it from Mark's perspective.

"On hearing of this, John's disciples came and took his body and laid it in a tomb. The apostles gathered around Jesus and reported to him all they had done and taught. Then, because so many people were coming and going that they did not even have a chance to eat, he said to them, 'Come with me by yourselves to a quiet place and get some rest.' So they went away by themselves in a boat to a solitary place. But many who saw them leaving recognized them and ran on foot from all the towns and got there ahead of them. When Jesus landed and saw a large crowd, he had compassion on them . . . So he began teaching them many things." Mk. 6:29-33

We see two things here - the sorrow of John's passing and the busyness of their ministry schedule that prevented them from stopping long enough to get something to eat. This sounds like a recipe for ministry burnout. Jesus then invited His disciples to get away somewhere quiet to rest. As soon as they started to move, they were seen, and a large crowd began gathering. Jesus, in the middle of His hunger, exhaustion, and sorrow, had compassion on them. Even in weariness and personal pain, He ministered, and the crowd grew to 5,000 men, besides women and children whom He taught for hours without a break. This would definitely violate current employment laws, which allow for a lunch break, and He would likely earn some days off for bereavement as well.

At the end of the day, the disciples came and spoke with Jesus. Remember, Jesus and the disciples hadn't had a chance to eat, because of their busy schedule. His disciples finally said, "'This is a remote place,' they said, and it's already very late. Send the people away so that they can go to the surrounding countryside and villages and buy themselves something to eat.'" Mk. 6:35-36

They were actually saying, "Hey Jesus, we're hungry. We haven't eaten all day. Can we stop ministering now?"

But Jesus answered them, "You give them something to eat." Mk. 6:37

What a statement! How preposterous this must have sounded. I can only imagine their look of disbelief. How in the *world* could Jesus require this of them? They hadn't eaten, and now He was asking them to feed 5,000 men, plus their families? They were dumbfounded, probably even offended. You can see it in their response. "They said to him, 'That would take eight months of a man's wages! Are we to go and spend that much on bread and give it them to eat?'" Mk. 6:37

Come on, Jesus; be realistic. It looked like Jesus had a blatant disregard for the well-being of His disciples. Not only was He *making* them minister when they were tired and hungry, but now He was also asking them to feed a multitude of people. I can only imagine the tone in their voices as they questioned Jesus about it.

Jesus replied by asking, "How many loaves do you have?" Mk. 6:38

Evidently, the disciples weren't sure that Jesus was serious. They were trying to figure out what Jesus wanted them to do. He spoke again to His bewildered disciples, and this time He put the question into an imperative. He says, "Go and see." Mk. 6:38

Off they went on what seemed like a fool's errand to see if any of the 10,000 had any food. I can just see them calling out, "Did anyone bring any food? Anyone?"

Sure enough, they found a boy who had five loaves, which were actually more like buns, and two fish.

They brought the boy's lunch to Jesus, and He directed them to arrange the people into groups and have them sit on the grass. Jesus then took the five loaves and two fish, gave thanks to God, and broke them. He then gave a small portion to each disciple, who would have had less than half a bun and about 1/6 of a small fish in their hands. Jesus instructed them to go and feed the people. What they had in their hand wouldn't have filled their own stomachs. They were each going to about 800 people, with a pittance of food in their possession. In the middle of their lack, the supernatural power of God was released.

With each piece they handed out, God did a miracle. He caused the portion they gave to be replenished. God didn't bring a dump truck of food – No, He wanted the disciples to participate in the miracle. He wanted to teach them faith. When they would give out of their own lack, it would release the miracle of fruitfulness. Now here is the end of the story.

"They all ate and were satisfied, and the disciples picked up twelve basketfuls of broken pieces of bread and fish." Mk. 6:42-43

Each disciple ended up with a full basket of food — more than enough to feed everyone, including themselves. The lesson wasn't about food. It was about releasing the supernatural miracle of Heaven in the middle of their own lack. The disciples eventually learned the lesson. After the Day of Pentecost, Peter, with James by his side, said to the crippled beggar at the temple gate, "Silver or gold I do not have, but what I do have I give you. In the name of Jesus Christ of Nazareth, walk." Acts 3:6

Peter had a revelation of what Jesus does in the middle of lack. He now had faith that God was able to do the impossible in any circumstance. He learned it that day while feeding the 5,000. The day started with John's death, great sorrow, and a busy schedule. He felt fatigue and hunger; but on that day, Jesus showed them the power of Heaven. God releases supernatural fruitfulness when we follow His word, care for others, and step out in faith.

We need to learn this lesson. It is time to move our focus off our own needs by giving thanks and putting our trust in a supernatural God. As we lay down our lives for others, God will supply the impossible. It is the seed that produces 30, 60, or 100 times what was sown. God is able to do more than we can think, ask or imagine. It's time we trusted Him to release the impossible in our midst.

CHAPTER 10

Humility and Success

God wants to use us to release the supernatural, but we should not overestimate our part in accomplishing it. We can easily slip into a wrong sense of pressure, thinking that the impossible depends on us. We must learn the difference between being a conduit and being the source. We have been given God's authority, dominion, Spirit, and power, but without Him, we can do nothing. Even Jesus only did what He saw the Father doing. There were times when Jesus could not do miracles because of the people's lack of faith. There are external factors that impact our ability to see the supernatural released; however, the impossible life should still be active and at work in us. How much it impacts the world around us is God's business; there are many factors outside our control.

Besides being a doer, I like to fix things – not so much mechanically, but if there is a situation that is less than ideal, I feel compelled to bring a solution. On one occasion, I was feeling the weight of the many things that needed fixing around me. As a citizen, I could see how much fixing our political situation needed. As a pastor, I could feel the weight of bringing the church out of its slumber and into God's powerful plan. As a parent, I saw the things that my kids needed to mature into, and last but not least, my house had several major repairs that needed attention. I had neither the time nor the resources to address them. I was beginning to sink under the pressure of it all.

I went for a walk in the woods behind my house, talking to the Lord about these things. I acknowledged my desire to see these areas change when suddenly, He spoke something I did not expect. He said, "Do you see all these trees around you? How long do you think they've been here?" I calculated that some trees were about 10-20 years old, but the biggest ones were probably more than 100 years old. Then, God said to me, "Some of these trees were here before you were born, and some will still be here after you die." It caught me off guard. Then, I began to understand His meaning. Here I was, feeling the weight of the world on my shoulders. I wanted to usher in the Kingdom of God and fix everything, yet these trees, which do nothing but grow, are a testament to the faithfulness of God. If trees can grow and stand tall without any laboring or striving, weathering decades of storms and winters, why was I so caught up striving to change what is beyond my control?

At that moment, I felt very insignificant in the big scheme of things. I imagine it was a similar sentiment to what David felt when he wrote these words: "When I consider your heavens, the work of your fingers, the moon and the stars, which you have set in place, what is man that you are mindful of him, and the son of man that you care for him?" Psalm 8:3-5 ESV

I realized that it was my pride that was triggering my sense of urgency. Too much of the solution depended on me – or at least that was my perspective. The truth is, God doesn't actually need me to change the world and usher in the impossible. God is quite capable of running the universe and unfolding His eternal plan without my great ideas or fix-it skills. So I repented to the Lord for my wrong perspective, I cast my cares upon Him, and suddenly the overwhelming sense of urgency was gone. It didn't matter if I changed the world – that was not my job. My role was to simply obey Him. God had used this moment to help humble me. Then, the grace of God began to flow. Peace replaced strife, hope replaced hopelessness, and strength replaced weakness.

It is important that we understand our place in God's plan. If it doesn't depend on me when it's going wrong, then it is not to my glory when it is going right. If God begins to use us to usher in the impossible, we may get an over-inflated sense of our own importance. We must first understand that God is not served by human hands, as if he needed anything (see Acts 17:25). The sooner we acknowledge that God invites us to partner with Him for our benefit, the better off we will be. This humility is key to walking in the supernatural power of the impossible life. God releases the impossible when we've exhausted our own solutions. When we reach the end of our rope, God's rope starts. That's when the impossible life begins. Our perspective needs to shift.

This also includes our understanding of success. Much of our world is success-driven. We see others prospering in life (with a good job, a nice family, a big house, and fancy vacations), and we categorize that as success. Perhaps, in part, that is success, but we tend to transpose that way of thinking onto the Christian life. We reduce the gospel to focus on personal blessings when those are byproducts, not the goal. Our metrics for measuring success are based on the world's standards. Even for church leaders, "success" generally has less to do with the presence and purpose of God than it does with making sure seats are filled and offerings are good. Many church leaders focus not on how to follow the leading of the Lord but rather how to grow a church in 5 easy steps because we think that bigger numbers mean we're successful. We've impacted more people with the gospel. But have we?

Jesus spoke to this after seeing rich people put large sums of money into the offering and a poor widow give one small coin. "Calling his disciples to him, Jesus said, 'Truly I tell you, this poor widow has put more into the treasury than all the others. They all gave out of their wealth, but she, out of her poverty, put in everything – all she had to live on.'" Mark 12:43-44

In Heaven's eyes, this widow's actions were more consistent with God's definition of worship and giving than those who gave large sums. Our value system is off. Speaking again about money, Jesus said, "'. . . You cannot serve both God and Money'. The Pharisees, who loved money, heard all this and were sneering at Jesus. He said to them, 'You are the ones who justify yourselves in the eyes of others, but God knows your hearts. What people value highly is detestable in God's sight.'" Luke 16:13-15

I wonder what success looks like in God's eyes. Was the man who had two talents and produced two more any less successful than the man who was given five talents and gained five more? God speaks to each of them identically, saying, "Well done, good and faithful servant" (see Mt. 25:21, 23). We measure success with a measuring stick of quantity, but God looks at the heart. He measures success with the measuring stick of quality. On the Day of the Lord, we will all have to give an account for how we have lived our lives. Our actions "will be revealed with fire, and the fire will test the quality of each man's work." 1 Cor. 3:13

We are then given rewards based on whether our life was built to God's glory or our own. We have to ask God to give us a new perspective on measuring success. We must understand that what is highly valued among men is detestable to God. Likewise, that which is discounted as insignificant by man is often held in high esteem by God. We have to decide what version of success we want to go after.

We have to recalibrate our hearts and minds to not judge by what our eyes see, or ears hear but to be led by the Spirit. God has us on a path designed for His glory. The path is a walk by faith and not sight, so we can't use the world's measuring tools as our compass. They will direct us away from where God is leading. This applies to our success-o-meter and our finance-o-meter. These are not what God values. Even our peace-o-meter can be faulty. The peace of God should rule in our hearts, but how often do Christians say, "I just don't have peace about that," when God is calling them to move outside of their comfort zone? The carnal mind will never feel peace when we are called to walk by faith. Our flesh goes crazy; the lawyer in our heads works overtime, ensuring that we don't have peace. It reminds us of every reason why we should not take a step of faith. We find ourselves calculating how much there is at stake. We must understand the difference between carnal peace and the peace that passes understanding. Our fleshly measuring tools of success, finances, and comfort cannot determine the right track with God. They're not designed for this journey.

That's why God gives us a guide. The Holy Spirit is our guide and teacher. He reminds us of everything that Jesus said (see John 14:26) so that we can walk the path of God. He leads us in truth and shows us Jesus, who is the way, the truth, and the life. When we submit, He becomes our teacher, trainer, and leader. Then we find that the impossible life is attainable, and we don't want to live anywhere else. It's where God dwells; it's the realm of the impossible. It's where He is calling you today. This is not because you are so extraordinary but because He is. God doesn't require extraordinary people; He will do extraordinary things through anyone who yields to Him completely. He is waiting for you to say 'Yes.' The more you say 'Yes' to God, the more extraordinary your life will be.

Humility is always the key. I encourage you to pray the dangerous prayer: "Lord, keep me humble." That's a prayer He is willing to answer. A day won't go by before you will have the opportunity to be humble. It is a gift because God resists the proud but gives grace to the humble. Our pride is our worst enemy. It will rob us of living the impossible life. If we refuse to be humble, God will eventually humble us, and that will feel like humiliation. However, if we yield to God and ask Him to keep us humble, then grace will surround us. His grace will define our lives and give us access to the power and presence of God.

Allow God to lead you today, and He will redefine your success. Put aside the world's measuring tools. Trust that God's ways for you are higher and better. Say 'Yes' to God and see what amazing things He has in store for you.

CHAPTER 11

You Can't Go It Alone

The best adventures in life are the ones we share with others. I mentioned earlier that I am a go-getter. I love to live fast. Everything I do, from eating to walking, is done with speed. I don't generally stop to smell the roses. I've got places to go and people to see. I come from a long line of fairly fast walkers. Thankfully, when I got married, despite being 6 inches shorter than me, my wife also liked to walk fast. This was most helpful, as we kept in step with one another. We went on walks, hikes, climbed mountains, and more.

When the kids came along, I discovered that my pace was not so helpful. When out for hike, I always like to see what's around the next corner. This drive, pulling me forward, was now leaving me separated from the rest of the family, who was now moving at the speed of the youngest child. On a few occasions, while adjusting to this new tempo, I would go around a corner and witness some incredible scene. I would see a bear running or a bird of prey catching a fish, but by the time the others caught up to me, the moment was gone. They missed it. I tried to explain to them what I had experienced, but my words always seemed to fall short.

Then, there were the moments that we experienced together as a family. One of the best things as a parent is to cherish the look on our children's faces as they take in the wonder of God's amazing world. Whether it is a glorious sunset or a massive wave crashing upon the shore, or rare wildlife sightings, these moments are much better when shared. They become the memories that weave through our lives and knit us more tightly together. "Remember when we . . ." is the start of some of my favorite conversations with my kids. Life is better when shared.

God has designed us to be part of community, to be a family, to be connected to one another. He reveals Himself as Father, Son, and Spirit. He is a relational God, and therefore His plan to make us in His image includes covenantal relationships. He has been relational for all eternity, and He made us for this very purpose.

The impossible life was never meant to be a solo journey. It is not just you and Jesus. We were always meant to be the family of God. Sure, some people seem to walk in a greater measure of supernatural power and grace, but they didn't get there alone. They had help along the way. The prophet Elijah walked in the impossible, and although he felt alone, God told him that he was actually one of 7,000 who was faithful (see 1 Kings 19). God gave him Elisha, and this was a great blessing to both men. When Jesus sent out His disciples to practice the impossible life, he sent them out two by two. The Bible says that one can put a thousand to flight, but two can send ten thousand fleeing (see Dt. 32:30).

Ecclesiastes 4:9-10 says two are better than one because they get a better return on their labor, and they can help one another. Jesus said where two or three agree, His presence and power are there in the midst of them (see Matthew 18:19-20). If we want to walk in the impossible, we will need to be connected with others. Spiritual synergism is powerful, and we cannot receive it unless we come together.

All of us need training and maturing, and no believer becomes mature by just reading their Bible and hearing God. We receive instruction and training through God-assigned mentors.

"Remember your leaders, who spoke the word of God to you. Consider the outcome of their way of life and imitate their faith." Heb. 13:7

We learn good and bad lessons by watching others. We discover what to do and what not to do. We are encouraged to imitate the faith of godly leaders. If you want to walk in the impossible, you need greater faith. Faith comes by hearing and hearing by the word of God (see Rom 10:17). Then, at some point, you must put into practice what you have learned. The training wheels need to come off, and when they do, you need guidelines to help you to stay on track. Scripture says that godly leaders will help you on this journey. We are to imitate and be inspired by their faith.

I remember a certain hockey fan in Vancouver. He had long hair and came to every Canucks' home game with a snare drum and drumstick. At various points throughout the game, he would stand up and begin to whip up the crowd, banging his drum and calling on the people to get up and support their team. Inevitably, his entire section began making noise, and then it would spread throughout the whole stadium. He earned the nickname "Crazy George." This man was not the focus of people's attention, but he was still able to affect an entire stadium. His passion and energy were contagious. This is what leaders do for us. They motivate us to get out of our seats. If you need more faith, get around people who are full of faith.

It will inspire you and cause you to see God in a bigger light and inspire you to live beyond your limitations.

The greatest blessings come from spiritual fathers and mothers. More than just cheerleaders, they lead us to maturity because they have walked the path before us. They bring inspiration and impartation. We may not realize the full effect a good spiritual father or mother is having on us, but years later, godly wisdom and character will blossom in our lives. One of the challenges of this generation is receiving from the older generation. There is a lack of discipleship, not because there are no fathers and mothers, but because people don't want others telling them what to do or how to live. When we undermine the process of allowing others to call us up and correct us, we miss becoming mature and will not walk in the fullness of the impossible life that God has for us.

There is another aspect of walking in the impossible, and it has to do with the fellowship of God's eternal plan. There is a principle in God's Kingdom that has to do with pushing forward together. The lack of unity is especially frustrating for people who are ready to charge ahead but are connected (by God's design) to others who will not move forward. We need a revelation of God's larger purpose. There will be limits to what a person, family, community, church congregation, region, and nation can experience in God. It is based not necessarily on the lowest common denominator but on the overall posture of the people. There are some things that can only be achieved together. This is God's design.

When Moses sent 12 men to spy out the Promised Land, they saw amazing produce and fruit. They saw incredible potential but also walled cities and giants in the land. Joshua and Caleb were full of faith; they believed in the promise of God and had no problem with giants. The other ten spies, however, were filled with fear and instilled that fear in the rest of the people. The nation's lack of faith caused them to wander for 40 years in the wilderness. It would have been tempting for Moses, Joshua, and Caleb to leave the rest behind, to reject the people's lack of faith, and go in the Promised Land alone. The Lord, however, didn't promise the land to just Moses, Joshua, and Caleb. They had an inheritance in it, but the land belonged to *all* of Israel. This had to be fought for and possessed corporately.

Sometimes we have a desire, calling, and even a word from God to move forward into the impossible life, but it doesn't seem to happen because others are not on board. Is it a timing issue? Is it a sin issue? These moments can be frustrating, but our job is to ensure we do not lose faith. We must focus on being ready when the time comes.

Do your part; you don't control others. Let God be God. Do what God has called you to do, but don't tear away from the relational setting God has placed you in. You need to understand that the community, nation, region, church, family, and marriage you are in all affect your ability to realize the purposes of God for your life. Sometimes it will pull you up. Other times, it will feel as if it is pulling you down. Don't give up! If Joshua and Caleb had gotten bitter about the lack of faith of the other spies and the nation who refused to enter, they would have missed out on their inheritance.

There is something bigger than our personal agenda that exists in the heart of God. In the wisdom and sovereignty of God, He has designed breakthroughs that require the agreement of others around us. He is a patient farmer who waits for the harvest of the earth. Our job is to not lose faith in the process but to keep holding on to the hope and promise of God until it comes to pass. The book of Hebrews speaks about this. After detailing the exploits and lives of many patriarchs and matriarchs, it says, "These were all commended for their faith, yet none of them received what had been promised since God had planned something better for us so that only together with us would they be made perfect." Heb. 11:39-40

Did you catch that? None of them received what had been promised because God planned something *better*, and this 'something' included us. Only together with us would they be made perfect. The word 'perfect' means complete. There are things in the heart of God that won't be complete unless they are experienced together with His people. That is God's design. He is a good Father with a big heart for all His people. He wants us to come to maturity and the fullness of His glory.

This will take a lot of time, trials, and tribulations. My encouragement to you today is to press into all that God has for you. Seek to live the impossible life. Pray for your family, church community, and nation. May you enter into all God has in His heart and mind for you, and may you do it together. The end of the story is exciting. It is filled with an outpouring of the supernatural power of God. We will see His people living the impossible life together.

CHAPTER 12

Life in the Spirit

When we think about people living out the impossible life, we usually think of Bible heroes who overcame insurmountable odds and performed miraculous acts. David and Goliath; Daniel in the lion's den; Elijah raising the dead; Esther rising to power, and Peter waking on water, are the stories many of us are familiar with. The problem is that we compare their reality to ours, and we think that what they lived is unattainable. The Scriptures give us accounts of amazing things, and we just assume that they happened to amazing people. The truth is, like any highlight reel, we aren't given the whole picture. Sure, we see miraculous moments, but we aren't given the details of the rest of their lives. The truth is, they were more like you and me than we realize. They had their good and bad days, maybe even good and bad years, filled with trials, failures, difficulties, and successes. Our heroes became extraordinary because of their faith in God and because of what God did on their behalf.

For some of us, it can seem totally beyond us; it is like reaching for the stars. About 120 years ago, it seemed impossible that man could fly. Sixty years ago, it seemed impossible that we could ever break through the atmosphere and explore space. Now we have people living on an international space station, and plans are underway for a manned mission to Mars. God has given humanity an amazing ability to dream and create. We are made in His image, but we're talking about living beyond what seems possible in the supernatural power of God.

There are physical laws that God has placed in nature, and they affect all of us. One of these laws is gravity. We know, by experience, that what goes up must come down. The universal law of gravity applies anywhere in the world. But if you escape the confines of earth and reach the outer limits of our atmosphere, then gravity changes.

It's not that the laws of gravity changed. After all, if you get closer to large objects like the moon or other planets, gravity again has its familiar effect. You can, however, experience total weightlessness when you go to space. What is impossible on earth is very possible outside of earth.

We often apply this to our Christian walk. We think that during this life, we have to live with the limitations of sin and weakness, but we understand that one day we will escape the confines of this realm and receive a resurrected life, one that is imperishable and incorruptible. We will be without sin and live forever with the Lord. In the meantime, most of us settle for an acceptable existence, trying to do good but not ever reaching for the impossible because it doesn't seem ... possible. The Bible, however, is full of people who touched the stars, so to speak. They experienced the impossible, and we can too.

One day, we will get the spiritual and physical upgrades that all creation groans and waits for, but don't miss the opportunity to experience the eternal, supernatural, impossible life of God right now. Why else would Jesus say to those who follow Him that they would do even greater things than He did? He was not talking about Heaven. He was talking about Heaven on earth. So, instead of just waiting for the next age, why not let God show us what weightlessness feels like now without going to space?

This is possible. The weightlessness of zero gravity that is experienced in space can also be experienced without ever going there. It can actually be achieved inside an airplane. It's called a parabolic flight. The pilot flies at G-Force one and maneuvers up and down at just the right angle and height over the course of a 10-mile run. The resulting effect creates about one minute of zero gravity conditions onboard the airplane. This is how some movies that are set in space are filmed. Astronauts appear to be weightless in the movie because they are. Zero gravity conditions have been created here on earth.

While the supernatural cannot be fully likened to a physical metaphor like this, I believe it illustrates how the impossible can become possible if the conditions are right. Some conditions for living the impossible life have been outlined in this book. Among them are wholehearted faith in God; living with abandonment; allowing God to work through our suffering and lack, waiting on God; remaining humble, and working with others. So, as the ups and downs of an aircraft can create conditions for the impossible (for zero gravity to take effect), so our unfailing trust in God creates conditions for the impossible as well. We need to let Him work in the ups and downs of life to release the supernatural. Even for the heroes of the faith, many of their breakthroughs did not come on the mountaintop, and they certainly didn't live there all the time. It's often in the valleys and trials that the supernatural power of God is released. We must learn to trust in God in the good times and the bad. Then we can live the impossible life.

We must tap into something greater than our finite understanding. Scripture tells us that the impossible happens "'not by might, nor by power, but by My Spirit' says the Lord Almighty." Zech. 4:6

The extent to which we live a life in the Spirit will determine our ability to walk by faith in the impossible. This is not just because the Spirit of God is able to release it but because walking in the flesh gets in the way of us experiencing the supernatural. Our flesh resists the things of God, rendering the impossible life out of reach. We must ask God to remove the focus of living according to our flesh and upgrade our limited knowledge. If we let Him work in our lives, we can soar in the Spirit. We can enter zero gravity conditions where we are free of the pulls and physical restrictions of the natural world. This type of life is only available through the Spirit.

Scripture says, "flesh and blood cannot inherit the kingdom of God, nor does the perishable inherit the imperishable." 1 Cor. 15:50

If we want to touch the things of God, we have to leave behind our earthly way of doing things, our need to know, and our need to control. When we give this control over to the impossible-working God, then everything becomes possible. The life of God becomes obtainable.

Jesus said, "The Spirit gives life; the flesh counts for nothing. The words I have spoken to you—they are full of the Spirit and life." John 6:63

In other words, our spiritual reality is more important than our physical reality; we just don't realize it. No matter what your eyes tell you, what your ears hear, or what the lawyer in your head may argue, God can and will make you an overcomer. And you don't have to feel strong to be an overcomer.

The apostle John, having received this revelation from Jesus, said, "You, dear children, are from God and have overcome them because the one who is in you is greater than the one who is in the world." 1 John. 4:4

He calls us 'dear children.' The power of the impossible, overcoming life is wrapped up in us becoming part of God's family. If you belong to Him, then scripture says His Spirit is in you. "For those who are led by the Spirit of God are the children of God." Rom. 8:14

If this is your reality, then you are no longer restricted to the confines of the flesh. If you are led by the Spirit of God, you can leave the flesh behind and live the impossible life now. Perhaps you are reading this and thinking that even though you are a Christian, you still battle with the flesh and with sin, and therefore you disqualify yourself from living a supernatural life. While the wages of sin is death, and sin does separate us from God, the blood of Jesus has triumphed. You are now hidden in Christ, so it's no longer you who lives but Christ who lives in you. It's His presence with you that you need. We try so hard to rid our lives of sin. We feel like God will never use us unless we get everything right. The truth is, we never will until Jesus returns. God will sanctify you and make you more like Christ, but that doesn't negate the fact that Christ is still dwelling within you.

Sinlessness is not the goal. If it was, Adam and Eve would have been perfect before the fall, but there was more in the heart of God. Adam and Eve were still corruptible. However, when resurrection day comes, they, and all who are in Christ, will receive an incorruptible life. So, we really need to redefine our definition of perfection. Perfection in your life is not just the absence of sin; it's the presence of God. It's the infilling of Himself. Together, with all God's people, we will be made complete, attaining to all the fullness of God.

Christ in us is the hope of glory. We belong to Him, and we are hidden in Christ. There is power in the name of Jesus. We have access to this power, but it's not our power. It's a universal law of physics that energy can be neither created nor destroyed, at least in the temporal universe we live in. It's the same with power - it cannot be created or destroyed - it can only be transferred. So, any power that we have doesn't start with us. Likewise, any power we lose due to our lack of faith or not living worthy of the call does not diminish or destroy the power of God. The Bible says, "But we have this treasure in jars of clay to show that this all-surpassing power is from God and not from us." 2 Cor. 4:7

God has released this power to us through the infilling of the Holy Spirit. Even in our imperfect state, our words and prayers have power when they are led by the Spirit and spoken in Jesus' name. We must be continually led by the Spirit to keep this power flowing. Paul asks, "After beginning with the Spirit, are you now trying to attain your goal through human effort?" Gal. 3:3 NIV 1984

We must remember that the impossible life is attainable only through the Spirit of God. Once we start living it, we must resist the temptation to think that we now possess this power independent of Him. If God grants you the power to do the impossible, it's not because you have proven so trustworthy or that you have received special status. The minute we fall into that trap, we need to go back and re-read chapter 10 of this book. We must remind ourselves that God gives grace to the humble. We remain focused on the Spirit of God, applying the word of God to our lives. We must be intentional, asking God to call us into something higher and greater than what we could ever be worthy of. We are jars of clay. God delights to fill us with His power because when we do the impossible, He is glorified. It's His power on display, not ours. It's His perfection on display, not ours. He alone is worthy of it all.

"Praise and glory and wisdom and thanks and honor and power and strength be to our God for ever and ever. Amen!" Rev 7:12.

Beyond the reaches of our earthly life is the realm of the impossible. One day, we will receive a glorified life, but until then, why not live the life God has provided? Why not experience zero-gravity conditions now? Your life of faith will release the supernatural power of God.

Have you given your life to Jesus? If so, you belong to Him, and His Spirit lives within you. Fan into flame the gift of God that is in you. You are called to do more than just witness miracles; you are called to perform miracles. Let the world experience the overflow of God in your life. You are made in the image of God, so put your faith in Him and step into the unknown. The impossible life is waiting.

www.ingramcontent.com/pod-product-compliance
Lightning Source LLC
Chambersburg PA
CBHW071900070526
44583CB00016B/1770